WORKPLACE ENVIRONMENT

Vs.

EMPLOYEE CHARACTERISTICS

Syed Nauman Ahmad

Abstract

Since employees are an integral part of any organization, it would be valuable for the organizations to observe how their workforce perceives things and behave in different working conditions. Personality-related characteristics of employees might affect their perception and performance. Therefore, comprehending the relationships among employees' personalities, workplace mistreatment, and job outcomes would be interesting and important for the organizations.

The study explores the said relationships among employee personality reflected through Islamic work ethics (IWE), workplace mistreatment (e.g. employees' perceived abusive supervision), and job outcomes (e.g. workplace deviance and prohibitive voice behavior).

The dissertation is composed of three empirical studies. In the first study, the relationship between IWE and abusive supervision is anticipated which is likely to be mediated by the Workplace Deviance (WD) of employees. In the second study, the impact of IWE on WD is expected which is projected to be moderated by abusive supervision and mediated by employees' hostility. While in the third study, a direct relationship between IWE and employees' Prohibitive Voice Behavior (PVB) is expected.

The data for these studies were gathered from 189 employees of various private sector organizations. For the study one and two, the data were analyzed using SPSS PROCESS. The mediating role of WD between IWE and perceived abusive supervision was confirmed in the first study. While the direct and indirect effects of IWE on WD were analyzed in the second study. In addition, the moderating role of employees' perceived abusive supervision between IWE and WD, and the mediating role of Employee Hostility (EH) between IWE and WD in the presence of abusive supervision were confirmed. In the last study, a simple linear regression model was run using SPSS to test and verify a direct and robust relationship between IWE and PVB.

The findings of the first study revealed a negative relationship between IWE and abusive supervision. In addition, the results verified that the proposed relationship was mediated by employees' WD. The results drawn from the second study showed a negative relationship between IWE and WD. Also, the moderating role of abusive supervision between IWE and WD was confirmed. Furthermore, the mediating role of employees' hostility in the relationship between IWE and WD was established. Finally, the findings of the third study validated a positive and strong relation between IWE and PVB. Employees possessing IWE demonstrated PVB.

The research contributes to expanding the abusive supervision and IWE related literature in the context of Pakistan. It identifies IWE, together with WD, as a new predictor of abusive supervision. Additionally, the relationship between IWE and WD, and IWE being a predictor of WD is identified. The relationship is moderated by abusive supervision and mediated by employee hostility. By challenging a widely held IWE-related research assumption, this study could also herald new avenues for future research. Moreover, it provides a better comprehension of employees' WD and PVB by verifying IWE as a predictor of both of these job outcomes.

Keywords: Islamic Work Ethics, Workplace Deviance, Abusive Supervision, Employee Hostility, Prohibitive Voice Behavior, SPSS PROCESS, Moderation, Mediation, Mediated Moderation, Pakistan.

Dedication

I dedicate this work
to the loving memory of
my late parents
and my family.

Table of Contents

List of Figures

List of Tables

List of Abbreviations

Symbol	Abbreviation
AMOS	Analysis of Moment Structures
BRI	Belt and Road Initiative
CFA	Confirmatory Factor Analysis
CFI	Comparative Fit Index
CPEC	China Pakistan Economic Corridor
DCT	Divine Command Theory
IWE	Islamic Work Ethics
PVB	Prohibitive Voice Behavior
RMSEA	Root Mean Square Error of Approximation
SOPs	Standard Operating Procedures
SPSS	Statistical Package for the Social Sciences
VPT	Victim Precipitation Theory
WD	Workplace Deviance

Chapter 1

Introduction

1.1 Introduction

An organization may be described as a group of persons collectively working to achieve a specific purpose. Given this definition, employees constitute an integral part of any organization. Their behavior and work could be a basis for a competitive advantage for the organization. Employee personality may be argued as a foundation of their behavior in the workplace. Each unique personality could lead an employee to perceive the existing state of affairs differently and behave accordingly. The organizations would like to understand the personality of employees which would enable them to better comprehend and predict behavior and quality of work of their employees. It would not be a surprise to see various individuals behave differently, even though they are working in the same environment. Therefore, it would be valuable for researchers and practitioners to explore why all employees do not behave in the same way, although they work in the same environment.

Two contributing factors that might explain employee's workplace behavior to be discussed in this dissertation are employee personality and employee perceptions. The unique personality characteristics of employees could influence their cognitive process. Moreover, perceptions of prevalent working conditions could affect their way of thinking. Both of these factors could compel employees to demonstrate a certain type of workplace behavior.

As the title of this dissertation suggests, this study explores relationships between the following main variables: employees' personality that is reflected through IWE of employees in the context of Pakistan; the workplace mistreatment described as employee's perceived abusive supervision (Tepper, 2000); and job outcomes. The job outcomes explored in the study are employees' workplace deviance (WD) and their prohibitive voice behavior (PVB). Employee Hostility (EH) is another variable that has been taken into consideration. The proposed relationships among these variables are being investigated in three independent empirical studies. The observed variables are briefly introduced in the following section.

Personality may be described as an individual's unique characteristic that explains the behavioral variation of that individual in certain situations. Understanding the nature of personality may help predict the behavior of that individual. Personality types of individuals could be thought of as predictors of their ethical or unethical behavior. Since individuals play an important role in organization, the conception of an individual's personality may also be applied in the workplace setting.

Employee personality has been researched to establish its role in the workplace. The review of the literature implies that employee personality could be a predictor of their work behavior and workplace-related job outcomes. Scholarly literature supports an obvious relationship between personality, behavior, and employee performance (e.g., Mowday & Spencer, 1981; Alarcon et al., 2009; Bowling & Eschleman, 2010; O'Neill et al., 2011; Henle & Gross, 2014).

Employees' work behavior could direct an organization toward planned or unplanned results. In either case, it would be crucial for an organization to predict and control job outcomes. Therefore, business managers would like to have a better insight into the personality of their employees to predict their behavior in the workplace. Understanding employee personality and workplace behavior could be very useful to envisage crucial job outcomes. Business managers would like to intensify the behaviors or actions of employees that lead to favorable job outcomes. At the same time, they would like to reduce or avoid such types of behaviors or actions of employees that lead to unfavorable job outcomes in the workplace.

Employee personality may be argued as being reflected through their work ethics. Some personality traits (e.g., neuroticism, agreeableness, and conscientiousness) are found to be positively related to ethical leadership behavior and ethical perception of individuals in the workplace (Kalshoven et al., 2011; Bratton & Strittmatter, 2013). According to these studies, work ethics possessed by employees and their subsequent workplace actions are associated with their various personality traits. Personality and work ethics of individuals are believed to be developed in the beginning years of an individual's life. Personality changes from one individual to another and has an incisive influence on behavior and attitudes of employees in the workplace (Saks et al., 1996; Caspi et al., 2005). Some studies confirm a clear link between some of the Big Five personality traits (agreeableness, openness, neuroticism, conscientiousness, and extraversion) and ethical perceptions of employees. Therefore, it may be argued that the ethics or work ethics of an individual can be considered as a dimension of personality. Employees' work ethics might follow a positive or a negative direction. Employee actions could be in accord with or against ethical standards established by their employers. It has been argued that a positive work ethic is a perfect antecedent of individuals' behaviors and attitudes in their future workplace (Porter, 2005; Mohammad et al., 2018). Ethics contributes to reducing counterproductive workplace behaviors (Sheehy, 1990). In this regard, Walker and Frimer (2007) show that a multitude of personality characteristics can help determine moral actions.

Ethics scholars have given special attention to religion as a main cause of an individual's work ethics (Murtaza et al., 2016). Personality and work ethics of individuals are believed to be developed in the beginning years of an individual's life which refers to a unique variable that changes from one individual to another and has a deep impact on employees' behavior and work attitudes (Saks et al., 1996; Caspi et al., 2005). Therefore, it would be justified to relate personality traits or work ethics of individuals to religion, especially in those cultures where it plays a dominant role (Khalid et al., 2020). As confirmed by Mohammad et al. (2018), Islamic work values are embedded in employee personality. Therefore, the personality of employees' may be revealed through their work ethics. Since the study is being conducted in the context of an Islamic society, it would be rational to relate Islamic work ethics (IWE) of employees as a reflection of their personality.

Scholars argue that IWE plays a key role in the workplace leading to organizational commitment, employee satisfaction, locus of control (Yousef, 2000a) and job loyalty (Ahmad, 2011). Employees belonging to an Islamic society are likely to possess IWE and would be less deviant from organizational standards or norms (e.g., Javed et al., 2019). While Arslan (2000) and Fifka (2013) contend that Protestant work ethics (PWE) influence the workplace-related values in many industrialized nations. Ali (1992) argued that PWE and IWE differentiate between positive and negative actions of employees in the workplace. So, both of these types of work ethics would likely promote ethical behavior, such as loyalty, sincerity, job dedication, teamwork, reliability, and determination in the workplace. This study is expected to contribute to the literature that deals with employee's ethical beliefs as antecedents of workplace deviance (e.g., Henle et al., 2005; Treviño et al., 2006). The workplace deviant behavior of employees may be considered as a deliberate behavior on the part of employees that violates organizational standards or norms and threatens the welfare of an organization or its members (Robinson & Bennett, 1995).

It may be argued that Islamic workplace values are drawn directly from the Qur'an and the Sunnah of the Holy Prophet Muhammad (May Allah have peace be upon Him and His Family, Qur'an, 4:59, Saheeh Al-Bukhari, Hadith No. 2072). These work values are likely to affect the thought process of employees who belong to an Islamic society. The characteristics of the society and culture affect organizations (Tayeb, 1997; Ali, 2005). In addition, righteous Islamic workplace-related values (e.g., cooperation, empathy, forgiveness, kindness, compassion, harmony) possessed by Malaysian employees are "embedded" in their personality (Mohammad et al., 2018). Therefore, it would be justified to reflect the work-related aspect of employees' personalities through their IWE in a society that consists of a predominantly Muslim population (e.g., Pakistan).

Business ethics could be thought of as the most important issue to be explored by business scholars (Ali, 2015). Various roles played by IWE will be discussed in three empirical studies of the dissertation. All of these roles seem to emerge from one of the central principles of Islam. This philosophical command has repeatedly been stated in the Holy Qur'an (e.g., Qur'an, 3:104, 3:114, 9:71).

... يَأْمُرُونَ بِالْمَعْرُوفِ وَيَنْهَوْنَ عَنِ الْمُنْكَرِ ...

This principle has been translated into English as "…enjoining what is right and forbidding what is wrong…" (Saheeh, 1997).

The next main variable to be explored is the perceived abusive supervision of employees. The perceived abusive supervision of employees is a reality in today's workplace and has adversely affected organizations (Li et al., 2016). It may be defined as employees' "subjective assessments" of the extent to which a supervisor is involved in "the sustained display of hostile verbal and nonverbal behaviors, excluding physical contact" (Tepper, 2000). It is explored in two different ways. First, employees' IWE has been proposed and investigated as a predictor of employees' perceived supervisory abuse. Second, the moderating role of employees' perceived abusive supervision, in the link between IWE and WD, is suggested and explored. Both of these roles of employees' perceived abusive supervision are discussed below.

In general, the research seems to consider perceived abusive supervision as an antecedent of various job outcomes (e.g., Tepper, 2000; Tepper et al., 2008 & 2009; Mitchell & Ambrose, 2007; Thau et al., 2009; Ferris et al., 2012; Javed et al., 2019). The study will align with scant literature that focuses on the antecedent of perceived abusive supervision (e.g. Artz et al., 2020). It could be useful for both researchers and practitioners to focus on those factors that lead to supervisory abuse. This could help them proactively minimize or avoid perceived abusive behavior in the workplace.

There are some personality characteristics or behaviors (e.g., negative affectivity; workplace deviance, unsatisfactory performance) that could make employees vulnerable to the abusive behavior of their supervisors (e.g., Bowling et al., 2010; Mawritz et al., 2017). To explore this relationship, it would be motivating to explore the function of IWE as an antecedent of employees' perceived abusive supervision. Employees who possess strong IWE would likely face a lower degree of abusive supervision because of their lesser inclination toward WD (see, for example, Syed & Azam, 2019). Therefore, the combination of IWE and WD could be thought of as a new mix of two antecedents that possibly can play a role in decreasing employees' perceived abusive supervision. This combination could lead to the lowering of employees' perceived abusive supervision. Thus, a mediating role of workplace deviance in the link between IWE and employee's perceived supervisory abuse is proposed and tested in one of the studies of this dissertation.

Another role played by employees' perceived abusive supervision is introduced in the following section. The moderating role of perceived abusive behavior of supervisors and, in the relationship between IWE and WD, through employee hostility, is proposed and investigated in this dissertation. Many researchers consider employees' perceived abusive behavior of supervisors as an injustice to employees or colleagues of these employees which causes negative behavior and unwanted outcomes (e.g., Zellars et al., 2002; Tepper, 2007; Ferris et al., 2012). Also, employees' perceived abusive supervision is linked to various unwanted workplace behaviors and job outcomes, including turnover intention, decreased employee self-esteem, workplace deviance, and decreased employee creativity (Ferris et al., 2012; Mathieu & Babiak, 2016; Liu et al., 2016).

The Holy Qur'an has introduced two antonym terms: "Adl" which means justice and "Zulm" which means injustice (Lewis, 2011). The same concept has been stated in the traditions of the Holy Prophet Muhammad (May Allah have peace be upon Him and His Family). The stated beliefs are expected to prepare members of the society to support fairness and justice and, at the same time, to fight against unfairness and injustice in society. Thus, these individuals would support justice or suppress injustice occurring in the workplace as well. Therefore, the workers, who possess a high degree of IWE due to their firmly held religious beliefs, would not tolerate injustice in the organization occurring in the form of perceived supervisory abuse. They would react or retaliate in the given situation.

Islamic teachings make employees fearless and encourage them to directly confront injustice. When their perceived abusive supervision is high, these individuals could retaliate in response. These employees are expected to retaliate strongly in this situation as compared to the ones who possess low or no IWE. So, to suppress injustice in the workplace, they would demonstrate hostility and deviance. Business managers would like to predict detrimental outcomes of this scenario (e.g. WD) when abusive supervisory behavior is demonstrated against employees who possess strong IWE. This prediction could enable them to proactively avoid, curb, or tackle these results.

Employees' workplace deviance (WD) is a variable that is also to be explored in the dissertation. It may be defined as a deliberate behavior on the part of employees that violates organizational standards or norms and threatens the welfare of an organization or its members (Robinson & Bennett, 1995). It has adversely affected organizations over time and has caused a "serious economic threat to organizations" when employees deliberately violate standards and threaten the interests of an organization or its members (Spector et al., 2006; Robinson & Bennett, 1995). Interpersonal injustice or workplace mistreatment leads to negative behaviors (Tepper et al., 2009; Mayer et al., 2012) because victimized employees reciprocate with workplace deviance (Duffy et al., 2002; Barclay et al., 2005; Mitchell & Ambrose, 2007).

Teachings of Islam instruct its followers to work with full sincerity and devotion to bringing good for them as well as for their organization and society (see, Ali, 1992; Ahmad, 2011; Murtaza et al., 2016). It may, then, be argued that the followers of the IWE are likely to stick to the course of action provided to them by their employers to efficiently bring good for the workplace and its members. Thus, they are expected to show a lower degree of workplace deviation (Javed et al., 2019). It would be relevant and valuable to explore employees' workplace deviance in the wake of employees' perceived abusive supervision and IWE. WD is explored in various models of study 1 and study 2 of the dissertation.

Employee hostility is another variable that is also explored in the study. It is described by Buss and Perry (1992), as a cognitive component of an individual's behavior that is linked with anger. After an arousal state of anger, some negative feelings developed in victimized employees will remain, causing bitterness and doubts about the intentions of the abusers (Buss & Perry, 1992). These feelings, caused by the thoughts of ill-will and injustice and doubts about the intentions of the abusers, can trigger hostile behavior amongst the offended employees. Mayer and colleagues (2012) argue that hostile effect caused by supervisor-referenced and subordinate-oriented mistreatment leads to employees' workplace deviance (Mayer et al., 2012). It may then be argued that individuals who possess strong IWE, upon facing or observing ill-will or injustice in the form of abusive supervision, might react and demonstrate hostile behavior. They could show workplace deviance when they perceive a high degree of injustice or supervisor referenced abusive behavior in the workplace. The effect of employee hostility, which comes into play in the wake of an increased level of abusive supervisory behavior in the relationship between IWE and WD, is to be investigated in the second study of this dissertation. The results could provide useful insights for the decision-makers that operate or plan to operate in Islamic countries. They would be able to make informed decisions concerning selection and recruitment of the right candidates for the right job in the organization.

Important job outcomes that are to be explored in this study are perceived abusive supervision of employees, employees' workplace deviance (WD), and their prohibitive voice behavior (PVB). Abusive supervision and workplace deviance have already been discussed above. The prohibitive voice behavior of employees is introduced in the following section.

The voice behavior of employees is described as verbally presenting suggesting solutions to solve problems in the workplace (Dyne et al., 2003). It has been argued by Liang et al. (2012) that voice behavior, in theory, could be an antecedent as well as a consequence of numerous psychological factors. The workplace voice is described as a verbal outcry of employees to express their concerns about practices and behavior of other employees, events, or the potentially harmful current state of affairs in the organization (Liang et al., 2012).

Surprisingly, the research so far has yet to focus on employees' IWE as a psychological predictor of the PVB. To fill this identified research gap, the third study of the dissertation proposes that an employee-specific psychological antecedent (e.g. IWE) would uniquely predict reports of employees' prohibitive voice behavior. This proposed relationship could be interesting for both researchers and practitioners and help them predict useful outcomes caused by employees' Islamic work ethics. The Islamic philosophy is expected to prepare its believers to support fairness and justice and, simultaneously, to fight against unfairness and injustice. These individuals, therefore, due to their strongly held religious belief, could retaliate against injustice in the workplace and are expected to strongly react and raise their voice. Therefore, the role of IWE as a predictor of PVB is proposed in the empirical study. Some interesting results are expected to follow that could contribute to expand the existing literature and help various stakeholders. Awareness concerning the PVB might proactively prepare business managers to mitigate or altogether avoid risks by creating or promoting a culture of whistleblowing in the workplace.

It could be imperative for scholars and practitioners to investigate the above-introduced variables in various exciting and valuable study models. These models have been tested and verified in three independent empirical studies. Some interesting and valuable results are expected to follow. A very brief introduction to these studies is given below.

Study 1 takes IWE, WD, and employees' perceived abusive supervision into account. The proposed role of employees' IWE and WD, in predicting perceived abusive supervision, is explored in this model of the study. It is empirically tested and verified that the Islamic work ethics of employees helps decrease perceived abusive supervision by decreasing their WD. By finding a new combination of two antecedents of employees' perceived abusive supervision, this proposition will contribute toward proposing a way to decrease perceived abusive supervision in the workplace. The said relationship will help business managers foresee valuable workplace-related outcomes that organizations would like to predict, observe, and keep in check. Besides helping practitioners, it will add value to IWE and perceived abusive supervision related to scant literature, especially in the context of Pakistan.

Study 1 confirms that IWE plays a role in decreasing perceived abusive supervision in the workplace. However, it would be interesting to explore what would happen when employees having IWE are exposed to abusive supervision. It could be useful for researchers and scholars to investigate how employees with strong IWE react and behave when the level of their perceived abusive supervision is high. How do these employees demonstrate their dislike or anger in the wake of an increased level of perceived abusive supervision? Would they always show a low or no WD in all types of situations or they would behave differently? Study 2 takes these thoughts into account. It introduces and tests the role of employee hostility when the relationship between IWE and WD is subjected to employees' perceived abusive supervision. Therefore, it is hypothesized in the study that the relationship between IWE and WD is moderated by employees' perceived abusive supervision and mediated by their hostility. Also, the indirect effect of IWE on WD, through employee hostility, would be significant when their perceived abusive supervision is high rather than low. This proposition will present some very useful and valuable results that could help business managers in several ways.

The models presented in studies 1 and 2 may be explained through the lens of the social exchange theory (SET; Homans, 1958) and the victim precipitation theory (VPT; Wolfgang, 1957). The role played by IWE on WD can be explained through social exchange theory (Homans, 1958), which argues that when social transactions between two parties occur, each party tried to increase benefits and decrease associated costs. Therefore, it may be argued that employees possessing high IWE will adhere to the course of action provided by their employer to efficiently bring good for the workplace and its members. Consequently, they are less inclined to deviate. Whereas, the relationship between IWE and employees' perceived abusive supervision, in the presence of WD, may be explained through the victim precipitation theory (VPT; Wolfgang, 1957). In the proposed model, WD is taken as employees' offensive behavior which triggers frustration and tension in their relationship with supervisors. Employees who possess strong IWE are less likely to deviate. Consequently, employing the VPT, it can be argued that less deviant employees will face a lower degree of perceived abusive supervision.

Another ancient meta-ethical theory may be applied as an underlying basis of all study models presented in the dissertation. As all of these studies discuss IWE, therefore the Divine Command Theory (DCT) could be employed to explain this set of religion-based workplace ethics. DCT, which may also be known as theological voluntarism, proposes that any action's standing as ethically good is established if it is heavenly commanded.

As stated above in this section, IWE is believe to be stemming directly from the Holy Qur'an and the Sunnah of the Holy Prophet Muhammad (May Allah have Peace be upon Him & His Family; Yousef, 2001). The workforce belonging to a Muslim society (e.g., Pakistan) is likely to follow IWE. Thus, IWE could be believed to qualify as ethically good to adhere to and practice in the workplace. It may be argued, therefore, that DCT is more comprehensive and encompassing to explain all of the studies.

Taking the argument further, the proposed model of study 3 is introduced in the following section. As observed in the second study, employees with strong IWE do not tolerate abusive supervision in the workplace. It is taken as an injustice by these employees and they retaliate and show hostile behavior to fight against it. If this argument is considered true, then employees with high IWE might also be concerned about other potentially harmful behaviors or events occurring in the workplace. This unique proposition will be explored in the third study. Therefore, this study proposes and tests a direct relationship between employees' IWE on prohibitive voice behavior (PVB) of employees. This is a relatively less explored job behavior of the workforce. The PVB is a voice behavior shown by employees to express their concerns about the potentially harmful existing circumstances in the workplace (Liang et al., 2012). It is interesting to find how IWE will impact the PVB of employees. It is hypothesized and confirmed in the study that a strong and positive relation between IWE and PVB of employees exists. This study contributes to the literature by introducing IWE as a new and useful antecedent of employee PVB. Thus, IWE has the potential to play its proactive role for the betterment of an organization. This study can benefit business managers in forecasting workplace behavior of individuals based on their work ethics.

Rice (1999) argues that Islamic ethics are believed to dictate economic activities, rather than the opposite. In addition, every action of a Muslim individual is gauged through the viewpoint of Islamic values and ethics (Khan et al., 2015). Therefore, this study model may be explained through the lens of Islamic values and ethics in a somewhat unique regional, religious, and organizational context of Pakistan. Findings of this study might be explained through social exchange theory (Homans, 1958), the norm of reciprocity theory (Gouldner, 1960), and the effective event theory (Weiss & Cropanzano, 1996).

Keeping in mind all of the discussed variables and proposed study models, the research aims of the dissertation are discussed in the following paragraph.

Overall, the study explores the relationships between employee's personality (i.e. IWE) and workplace mistreatment, and its impact on two important job outcomes. The overall research has been divided into three interlinked but independent studies. The first study aims to examine the relationship between IWE and employees' perceived abusive supervision, which is mediated by WD. The focus of the second study is on exploring the relation between Islamic work ethics and workplace deviance which is moderated by employees' perceived abusive supervision and mediated by their hostility. The third study investigates the relationship between employees' IWE and prohibitive voice behavior.

The structure of the dissertation will be described in the following section.

1.2   Structure of Dissertation

This dissertation has four distinct chapters. Chapter 1 introduces the purpose and significance of all the study variables to be explored in the dissertation. These variables are to be explored in various interesting study models. The introduction of these study models is also a part of chapter 1. The research aims of all these empirical studies are presented toward the end of the chapter.

Chapter 2 includes a detailed review of literature of all three empirical studies. The theoretical lenses applied in these studies are also discussed in this chapter. Observed variables are reviewed concerning antecedents and precedents of employees' personalities, reflected through their workplace ethics (i.e. IWE) and job outcomes. The theoretical underpinning of all three studies is also discussed. This review of the literature leads to develop proposed models and hypotheses of all three empirical studies.

Chapter 3 explains the research methods adopted to conduct all three studies. This chapter starts with an explanation and justification of the theoretical standpoint taken for the research. Details about sampling, sample characteristics, data collection methods, types of organizations selected for data collection, and ethical considerations are discussed. Then the chapter discusses the scales and constructs that were employed to measure study variables. The confirmatory factor analysis (CFA) was performed to empirical test the validity and reliability of the employed scales. Furthermore, this chapter gives the test results and analyses. The proposed models and hypotheses of the first and the second study were tested using regression analysis in PROCESS SPSS. To test the proposed model and hypothesis of the third study, simple linear regression analysis was run using SPSS. Also, a detailed discussion regarding tests results is also provided in this chapter.

Finally, Chapter 4 is dedicated to the conclusions from the studies, future research directions, and managerial implications of each study. In the end, this chapter presents contributions made, limitations and potential opportunities of subsequent research. The bibliography and some important appendices are presented at the end of the dissertation.

1.3   Chapter Summary

Chapter 1 introduces the research conducted. First, the background and significance of the study are discussed. Then, the variables explored in the study are introduced. Also, the research aims are briefly introduced. This section is then followed by an overview of the overall structure of each study conducted. A summary of each chapter is also included here.

The next chapter, Chapter 2, presents a detailed review of the literature and theoretical foundations of all three studies. This will lead to the development of the theoretical models and hypotheses of each study.

Chapter 2

Literature Review

2.1 Introduction

In the previous chapter, Chapter 1, it was argued that relationships among three main variables exist. The variables under consideration are: Islamic work ethics (IWE), employees' perceived abusive supervision and job outcomes (WD & PVB). This chapter reviews the relevant literature to find evidence to support the proposed arguments.

The first section of this chapter is about Study 1. This study reviews the role of IWE in shaping the behavior of individuals in the workplace. It is argued that a negative relationship exists between IWE and WD. So, the literature suggests IWE-inclined employees comply with the instructions provided to them by their organizations. This leads to a lower degree of WD amongst employees who possess strong IWE. Furthermore, in the same section of the chapter, the relationship between IWE and employees' perceived abusive supervision, in the presence of WD as a mediator, is discussed. It is argued that IWE, together with WD, plays a role in reducing employees' perceived abusive supervision. Thus, both IWE and WD act as antecedents of employees' perceived supervision.

The second section of the chapter talks about the Study 2. This study reviews the role played by employees' perceived abusive supervision and hostility in the relationship between IWE and WD. It is argued that the relationship between IWE and WD is moderated by employees' perceived abusive supervision. In addition, it is argued that at a certain level of employees' perceived supervision, employees' hostility emerges and mediates the same relationship.

Finally, the third section of the chapter provides evidence in support of the relationship between IWE and prohibitive behavior of employees (PVB). The results suggest a strong and positive relationship between IWE and PVB.

The discussion in these sections of the chapter leads to the development of relevant research models and hypotheses.

A detailed review of the literature related to these main variables is presented in the following three studies. These variables are Islamic work ethics, workplace deviance, and perceived abusive supervision of employees.

2.2 Study 1: Islamic Work Ethics and Workplace Deviance: Antecedents of Abusive Supervision

The literature related to Islamic work ethics and workplace deviance is reviewed in the following sub-section of the study.

2.2.1 Islamic Work Ethics and Workplace Deviance

Workplace-related Islamic teachings may directly be traced from the Qur'an and the Sunnah of the Holy Prophet Muhammad (May Allah have peace be upon Him and His Family). The Qur'an supports constructive behavior through creating discipline and respect for hierarchical order by stating that "O People who Believe! Obey Allah and the Noble Messenger and those amongst you who are in authority…" (Qur'an, 4:59). The Holy Prophet Muhammad (May Allah have peace be upon Him and His Family) is reported to have said, "Nobody has ever eaten a better meal than that which one has earned by working with one's own hands. The Prophet of Allah, David (May Allah have Peace be upon Him & His Family) used to eat from the earnings of his manual labor" (Saheeh Al-Bukhari, Hadith No. 2072). Believers of Islamic guidelines will bring good for themselves, their organization and society (Ahmad, 2011; Murtaza et al., 2016). Employees belonging to an Islamic society are likely to possess IWE and would likely be less deviant (e.g., Javed et al., 2019). Considering this philosophy, it could be expected that employees with higher IWE would show complete loyalty and commitment toward their employer and thus would be less deviant.

Researchers who have studied IWE have usually pointed out its positive contribution toward job outcomes (e.g. Moayedi, 2009; Rokhman, 2010; Haroon et al., 2012; De Clercq et al., 2018). Recently, a similar positive contribution of IWE in reducing the impact of supervisory abuse on WD was also verified by Javed and his colleagues (2019). In conformity with the literature, it would be justified to anticipate a positive relationship between IWE and WD.

WD adversely affected organizations and caused a "serious economic threat to organizations" (Spector et al., 2006; Bennett & Robinson, 2000). Through WD, employees deliberately violate standards, and threaten the interests of their employers or their employees (Robinson & Bennett, 1995).

Aligning with similar studies (e.g., Javed et al., 2019), it is argued that followers of IWE will show full sincerity and devotion toward their employer and will stick to the prescribed course of action with an intention to bring good for the organization and its members. So, they would show less deviation from the standard operating procedures (SOPs).

The relationship between IWE and WD may be explained with the help of social exchange theory (SET), proposed by Homans in 1958, which states that when social transactions between two parties occur, each party tries to increase benefits and decrease associated costs. It may be argued that employees possessing high IWE would adhere to the given course of action with the intention of efficiently bringing good for the workplace and its members. Therefore, these employees would be less inclined toward WD. Considering the above discussion, the following hypothesis is proposed:

Hypothesis 1: Islamic work ethics are significantly and negatively related to workplace deviance.

The literature related to employees' perceived abusive supervision and workplace deviance is reviewed in the following sub-section of the study.

2.2.2 Employees' Perceived Abusive Supervision and Workplace Deviance

The perceived abusive supervision of employees may be defined as employees' "subjective assessments" of the extent to which a supervisor is involved in "the sustained display of hostile verbal and nonverbal behaviors, excluding physical contact" (Tepper, 2000). Abusive supervision is a reality in the workplace and has adversely affected organizations (Li et al., 2016).

Generally, the literature has focused on perceived abusive supervision as an antecedent of negative job-outcomes (e.g., Tepper, 2000; Mitchell & Ambrose, 2007; Tepper et al., 2008; Tepper et al., 2009; Thau et al., 2009; Ferris et al., 2012; Javed et al., 2019). However, this study will be in conformity with somewhat scant literature that has dealt with antecedents of perceived abusive behavior of supervisors (Khan et al., 2017). It would be useful for researchers and practitioners to predict workplace damaging behaviors and outcomes, so they may proactively avoid such occurrences.

In accordance with the previous research, it may be argued that some personality characteristics (e.g., negative affectivity; workplace deviance) could make employees vulnerable to abusive behavior of supervisors (e.g., Bowling et al., 2010; Mawritz et al., 2017). Utilizing victim precipitation theory, proposed by Wolfgang in 1957, this study may become a part of the literature that highlights supervisory abuse caused by employees' personality or behavior (e.g., Aquino & Douglas, 2003).

Scant research was found in the literature that explored IWE and WD as predictors of perceived supervisory abuse. It may be argued that since individuals with high IWE engage in less workplace deviance, IWE would therefore play a role in reducing perceived supervisory abuse. So, by exploring and confirming IWE and WD as antecedents of perceived supervisory abuse, this study would add value to the literature on IWE and the stated employees' perceived abusive behavior of their supervisors.

Employing victim precipitation theory, proposed by Wolfgang (1957), Henle and Gross

(2014) argued that employees possessing certain personalities or emotions are believed to face more abusive supervision, as these characteristics might activate hostility and frustration in their supervisors. A low degree of employees' conscientiousness or emotional instability was considered offensive personality traits that increased the likelihood of hostility and tension in their relationships with others (Kim & Glomb, 2010). Making use of victim precipitation theory, WD might be taken as an offensive behavior on the part of employees which could trigger the likelihood of hostility, frustration, and tension in their relationship with supervisors (Henle & Gross, 2014). Therefore, deviant employees could face more abusive supervision. In contrast, it may be justified to argue that less-deviant employees would face a low degree of supervisory abuse.

As stated above in the introduction section of the dissertation, IWE directly originate from the Holy Qur'an and the Sunnah of the Holy Prophet Muhammad (May Allah have Peace be upon Him & His Family; Yousef, 2001). So, in the light of the Devine Command Theory (DCT), it may be argued that the workforce belonging to a Muslim society (e.g., Pakistan) is likely to adhere to IWE. Furthermore, if followers of IWE demonstrate a low degree of workplace deviance, these employees are expected to face low perceived abusive actions, decisions, or behaviors of their supervisors. Hence, employees possessing strong IWE would face low abusive supervision because of their lower inclination toward WD.

Based on these arguments, the following two additional hypotheses may be suggested.

Hypothesis 2: Workplace deviance is significantly and positively related to employees' perceived abusive supervision.

Hypothesis 3: The relationship between Islamic work ethics and employees' perceived abusive supervision is mediated by workplace deviance.

Figure 1 demonstrates the theoretical model of the study 1. This model illustrates a relationship between IWE and employee perceived abusive supervision, mediated by WD.

Figure 1

Conceptual Model of Study 1

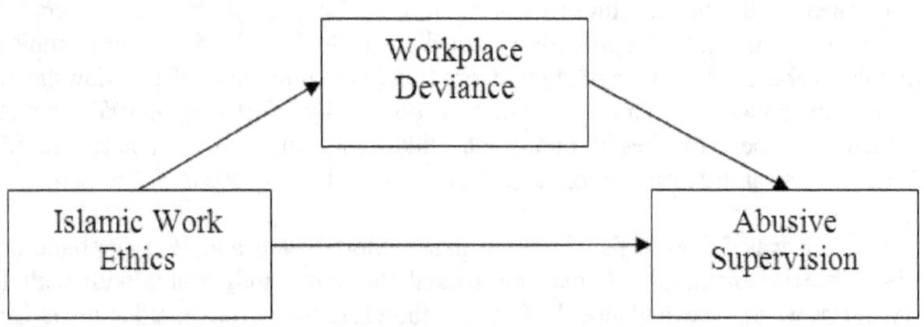

A detailed review of the literature related to four main variables is presented in the following study. These variables are: Islamic work ethics, workplace deviance, perceived abusive supervision of employees, and employees' hostility.

2.3 Study 2: Islamic Work Ethics and Workplace Deviance: Moderated by Abusive Supervision and Mediated by Employee Hostility

The literature related to Islamic work ethics and workplace deviance is reviewed in the following sub-section of this study.

2.3.1 Islamic Work Ethics and Workplace Deviance

Islam is the second-largest religion of the world, after Christianity, and more than one-fifth of the total population of the world is Muslim (Maoz & Henderson, 2013; Johnson & Grim, 2013; Minhat & Dzolkarnaini, 2016). Religion is a major source of work ethics (Murtaza et al., 2016). Teachings of Islam have urged its followers to work with full sincerity and devotion to their employer (Ali, 1992). Rice (1999) stated that as the Holy Qur'an guided in all aspects of human life, some ethical principles may be drawn from it (e.g., work quality, seeking knowledge, satisfying trust and workplace requirement, giving full quantity and weight). By affecting thoughts and consequent actions, followers of this philosophy were to bring good for themselves, for their organization and society (Ahmad, 2011; Murtaza et al., 2016). So, Islam is a natural contender to be explored for its work ethics and it is expected to provide unique work ethics.

While differentiating IWE from PWE, Yousef (2000b) argued that IWE placed more stress on intentions than results. Also, Yousef (2001) stated that IWE derived its origin directly from the Holy Qur'an (a book believed by Muslims as the statements of Allah, the God) and the Sunnah (authentic and recorded sayings, traditions and practices of the Holy Prophet Muhammad; May Allah have Peace be upon Him & His Family). Islamic teachings were categorized into two parts that required an individual's actions to be according to the will and pleasure of Allah (Abuznaid, 2009; Javed et al., 2019). The first part was related to all actions towards Allah alone. The second part, building good relationships with fellow human beings for the sake of Allah's pleasure (Javed et al., 2019), was to provide the foundation of IWE.

Yousef (2000b & 2001) investigated the mediating role of organizational commitment between IWE and employee behavior and the moderating role of IWE between employees' job satisfaction and commitment. Uygur (2009) studied IWE and entrepreneurs' behavior within their organizations. Another study (Ali & Al-Owaihan, 2008) explored IWE in the context of political, cultural and religious perspectives related to organization and management. The relationship between IWE and workplace deviance (Golparvar & Nadi, 2011) and between Islamic spirituality and workplace deviance was also explored (Bhatti et al., 2016). The role of IWE as a mediator between trust development and contributor to knowledge sharing was investigated by Mursaleen and colleagues (2015).

Continuing with the same trend, some recently conducted studies investigated the impact of IWE on helping behavior, citizenship behavior of employees and their work engagement, employees' attitudes and behavior in terms of perceived organizational justice, psychological ownership, and employees' performance (Mohammad et al., 2018; De Clercq et al., 2019; Farid et al., 2019). From an analysis of these studies, it may be inferred that a general belief held by the IWE researchers is that the role played by IWE or the relationship between IWE and job outcomes would always follow a certain predictable direction. However, by challenging this supposition, it may be argued that there could be some situations when the role played by IWE or the relationship between IWE and job outcomes would demonstrate unpredictable results. This study then tests the stated assumption by exploring the link between IWE and employees' workplace deviance in the presence of two very important variables.

Workplace deviance is a deliberate employee behavior that violates organizational standards or norms and threatens the welfare of an organization or its members (Robinson & Bennett, 1995). It has affected organizations for a long time (Spector et al., 2006). Interpersonal injustice or mistreatment has been considered as an antecedent of workplace deviance and negative behaviors in the workplace (Tepper et al., 2009; Mayer et al., 2012). Victimized or mistreated employees in the workplace have usually reciprocated with negative behavior (Duffy et al., 2002; Barclay et al., 2005; Mitchell & Ambrose, 2007). In a recently conducted study, Javed and colleagues (2019) explored the impact of abusive supervision on workplace deviance. The study is expected to be aligned with the research that has considered the ethical belief of employees as an antecedent of workplace deviance (e.g., Henle et al., 2005; Treviño et al., 2006).

However, the teachings of Islam urged its followers to work with full sincerity and devotion to bringing good for themselves as well as for their organization and society (see, Ali, 1992; Ahmad, 2011; Murtaza et al., 2016). Another study verified the moderating role of IWE between employees' perceived abusive supervision and workplace deviance (Javed et al., 2019). Employees possessing a higher degree of IWE would respect and appreciate their leader in the workplace and both leaders and followers must be considered as brothers (Mohammad & Quoquab, 2016). It can be argued that the followers of the IWE, while showing full sincerity and devotion toward their employer, would stick to the course of action provided to them by their leader, supervisor or employer with an intention to efficiently bring good for the workplace and its members. Consequently, they would be less inclined to deviate from the standard operating procedures (SOPs) prescribed to them by their employer. On the basis of these arguments, it may be hypothesized that subordinates who possess strong Islamic work ethics are less inclined toward workplace deviance than those without such ethics. Therefore, the following hypothesis may be proposed:

> Hypothesis 1: Islamic work ethics are significantly and negatively related to workplace deviance.

In an attempt to find a possible link between these variables, the literature related to employees' perceived abusive supervision, hostility and deviance in the workplace is reviewed in the following sub-section of the study.

2.3.2 Employees' perceived abusive supervision, Employees' Hostility and Workplace Deviance

Employees' perceived supervisory abuse may be described as their "subjective assessments" of "the extent to which supervisors engage in the sustained display of hostile verbal and nonverbal behaviors, excluding physical contact" (Tepper, 2000).

Mathieu and Babiak (2016) reported a positive and strong relationship between corporate psychopathic, abusive supervision and turnover intentions. Interpersonal injustice decreases employee self-esteem and increases predicted deviant workplace behavior (Ferris et al., 2012). Employee creativity is believed to be negatively affected by perceived abusive supervision (Liu et al., 2016). Employees persistently facing abusive supervision are more prone to show psychological distress (Tepper, 2000). Perceived abusive supervision has been positively linked with workplace deviance (Javed et al., 2019). All of the above-stated studies have suggested that, in general, perceived abusive supervision is linked to damaging workplace behaviors and job outcomes. Managers would like to predict these harmful occurrences in the workplace, to proactively avoid, curb or tackle these untoward confrontations in the workplace.

Many researchers have affirmed abusive supervision as injustice or leading to injustice in the workplace, causing negative behavior and job outcomes (e.g., Zellars et al., 2002; Tepper, 2007; Ferris et al., 2012). Khan and colleagues (2015) argued that some constructs (e.g., worldviews of individuals, their submission to authorities and work performance) might be considered as antecedents of employees' perception of abusive supervision. This study would align with the research which has investigated the impact of employees' perception as a predictor of job outcome.

Recent research (De Clercq et al., 2018) confirmed a positive role played by the IWE in promoting supportive behavior amongst employees when they were subjected to abusive supervision. Deriving its roots directly from the Holy Qur'an and the Sunnah of the Prophet Muhammad (May Allah have peace be upon Him and His Family; Yousef, 2001), it may be stated that the Islamic teachings stress establishing justice, fairness, equality while eradicating injustice, oppression, and inequality from society.

The Holy Qur'an introduced two antonym terms: "Adl" and "Zulm" (Lewis 2011). Thus, the believers would either support "Adl" i.e. justice or suppress "Zulm" i.e. injustice. It was stated in the Holy Qur'an that "O you who believe, stand up as witnesses for God in all fairness, and do not let the hatred of a people deviate you from justice. Be just: This is closest to piety, and beware of God. Surely God is aware of all you do" (Qur'an, 5:8). The similar concept was repeatedly stressed in the Holy Qur'an (Qur'an, 16:90). Maintaining the same viewpoint, the following tradition of the Holy Prophet Muhammad (May Allah have peace be upon Him and His Family) stated that God spoke to Him in this manner "My slaves! I have forbidden injustice for Myself and I have made it forbidden among you, so do not wrong one another…." (Saheeh Al-Bukhari, Hadith No. 490). Moreover, the Holy Prophet Muhammad (May Allah have peace be upon Him and His Family) has been reported to have said: "Indeed, among the greatest types of Jihad is a just statement before a tyrannical ruler" (At-Tirmidhi, Hadith No. 2174). Furthermore, another tradition of the Holy Prophet Muhammad (May Allah have peace be upon Him and His Family) stated: "He who amongst you sees something abominable should modify it with the help of his hand, and if he has not strength enough to do it, then he should do it with his tongue, and if he has not strength enough to do it, (even) then he should (abhor it) from his heart, and that is the least of faith" (Sahih Muslim, Hadith No. 49a).

This stated philosophy is expected to prepare its believers to support fairness and justice and, simultaneously, to fight against unfairness and injustice. These individuals, due to their strongly held belief, would likely possess strong IWE. These teachings, while making employees fearless, would encourage them to directly confront injustice. Such individuals would retaliate against injustice or supervisor referenced abusive behavior. Therefore, they would confront more strongly and show hostility as compared to ones with low or no IWE.

Hostility maybe described as a cognitive component of an individual's behavior (Buss & Perry, 1992). While establishing a link between anger and hostility, Buss and Perry (1992) argued that after the arousal state of anger, some negative feelings developed in victimized employees will remain, which would cause bitterness and doubts about the intentions of the abusers. Perception of hostile behavior would trigger when there were thoughts of ill-will and injustice amongst the victimized employees.

Hostile effects caused by supervisor-referenced and subordinate-oriented mistreatment leads to employee workplace deviance (Mayer et al., 2012). It may be argued that the individuals who possessed high IWE might demonstrate hostile behavior at a certain level of abusive supervision. They would show workplace deviance when they perceived the occurrence of unjust or supervisor referenced abusive behavior in the workplace that was against their belief system.

It was observed that IWE was negatively related to workplace deviance (Ahmad & Omar, 2014; Bhatti et al., 2015; Bhatti et al., 2016; Javed et al., 2019). But, if the behavior of Muslim employees did not coincide with the previous research findings, it may be explained through a key concept of "enjoining what is right and forbidding what is wrong" .This concept is repetitively stated in the Holy Qur'an (e.g., Qur'an, 3:104, 3:110 & 3:114), and was reiterated in the following tradition of the Holy Prophet Muhammad (May Allah have peace be upon Him and His Family) that stated: "By Him in Whose Hand my life is, you either enjoin good and forbid evil, or Allah will certainly soon send His punishment to you. Then you will make supplication and it will not be accepted" (At-Tirmidhi, Hadith No. 193).

Leader mistreatment, workplace injustice or abusive behavior could cause feelings of stress and hostility amongst the victimized employees. It would not be a surprise if victimized employees with high IWE and hostility demonstrated workplace deviance. Due to their firm belief, they might demonstrate resilience to forcefully confront and oppose perceived abusive supervision. They might be sensitive towards abusive supervision which would cause hostility and eventually deviance (Mayer et al., 2012). Therefore, the followers of IWE might directly and forcefully confront transgressors with an intention to play their constructive role and to bring good to the workplace. They might react due to their perceived tyranny, injustice, or abusive supervision in the workplace by demonstrating workplace deviance. This behavior may be explained by employing the norm of reciprocity theory. It might be proposed that when employees with high IWE are subjected to abusive supervisory behavior, they are expected to retaliate in return as directed by Islamic principles and predicted by theories of human behavior, still with an intention to bring good for the workplace and its members. As a result, they are likely to deviate from the guidelines provided to them by their abusing supervisors.

Therefore, in the presence of employees' perceived abusive supervision, it may be predicted that strong employee workplace deviance will be shown by hostile victimized employees. In the light of these arguments and by following a similar empirical study conducted by Khan and his colleagues (2018), the following hypothesis, which has two parts, may be proposed.

Hypothesis 2: Employee perceived abusive supervision moderates the indirect effect of IWE on workplace deviance through hostility. The indirect effect of IWE on workplace deviance through hostility is significant when employees' perceived abusive supervision is high rather than low.

Figure 2

Conceptual Model of Study 2

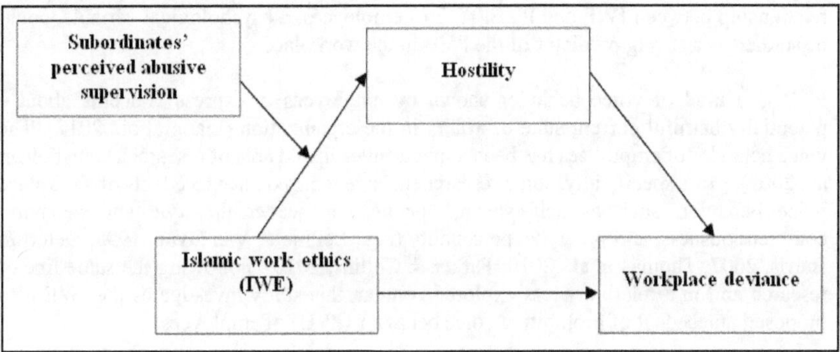

The conceptual model of study 2 is shown in Figure 2. The model links IWE, as an antecedent, with workplace deviance. The said relation between IWE and workplace deviance is moderated by employee perceived abusive supervision and mediated by their hostility. These proposed relationships will be analyzed and tested in Chapter 3.

A detailed review of the literature related to two variables is conducted in the following section. The variables under consideration include Islamic work ethics and prohibitive voice behavior of employees.

2.4 Study 3: Islamic Work Ethics and Employee Voice Behavior

An interesting role of IWE, in the presence of WD, as an antecedent of employees' perceived abusive supervision, is proposed in study 1 of the dissertation. The proposed role could help in predicting employees' perceived abusive supervision. It is argued that employees with strong IWE perceive a lower degree of abusive supervision because of their lesser inclination toward WD (see, for example, Syed & Azam, 2019). Therefore, IWE and WD can be considered as a new combination of two variables that could decrease employee's perceived abusive supervision.

To take this argument further, it would be interesting to explore how employees with high level of IWE will behave if level of their perceived abusive supervision does not decrease but increases beyond a certain level. It would be useful to discover how these employees demonstrate their dislike when they face an increased level of perceived abusive supervision. Study 2 takes into account these thoughts and introduces the role of employee hostility when employees with IWE face increased level of abusive supervision. It is argued that employees with IWE do not withstand injustice in the form of abusive supervision in the workplace, considering it harmful for employees and work environment, and they retaliate. If this argument is true, then the same employees should be similarly concerned about other types of potentially harmful happenings in the workplace. Keeping this rationale in view, an impact of IWE on voice behavior of employees is proposed in study 3. This study proposes and tests a direct relation between IWE on a relatively less explored job behavior i.e. prohibitive voice behavior (PVB) of employees. It would be interesting to confirm and explore the nature of the proposed relationship between IWE and PVB. IWE of employees, a psychological variable, could be studied as a strong predictor of the PVB in the workplace.

PVB is a kind of voice behavior shown by employees to express concerns about a potentially harmful current state of affairs in the organization (Liang et al., 2012). The voice behavior of employees has been a much-investigated area of research (Brinsfield et al., 2009). More specifically, some researchers have focused on antecedents of workplace voice behavior, such as self-esteem, openness in leadership style and behavior, conscientiousness, and proactive personality (e.g., LePine & Van Dyne, 1998; Detert & Burris, 2007; Thomas et al., 2010; Parker & Collins, 2010). Following the same line of research and in a relatively less explored context, this study investigates the IWE as a proposed antecedent of prohibitive voice behavior (PVB) of employees.

The review of literature was unable to identify any research that studied IWE as a predictor of the PVB. IWE is a relatively less recognized psychological antecedent of employee voice behavior and that too, in the context of an Islamic country like Pakistan. Therefore, the effect of IWE on PVB of employees is observed in this study. The study thus bridges the identified research gap and suggests the role of IWE as an antecedent of voice behavior or whistleblowing in the workplace. It could be valuable for decision makers to study the proposed relationship to help them predict workplace voice behavior of workforce in the context of Pakistan.

The results of the study might be explained through social exchange theory (Homans, 1958), the norm of reciprocity theory (Gouldner, 1960) and the affective event theory (Weiss & Cropanzano, 1996).

In order to explore a possible link between two main variables of the study, a detailed review of the literature is conducted in the following section of the study. The variables under consideration include Islamic work ethics and prohibitive voice behavior of employees.

2.4.1 Islamic work ethic (IWE) and Prohibitive Voice Behavior (PVB)

Recent growth in international trade and globalization caused mainly by a marked reduction in transportation and communication costs (Chase-Dunn et al., 2000), has created an opportunity for many organizations to expand their business operations beyond their national boundaries. Many religions are followed and practiced in different parts of the world (Parboteeah et al., 2009). Therefore, recent business expansions have enhanced the need to better understand other religions and cultures (Rice, 1999) of the world.

Business ethics scholars have given special attention to religion as it is considered a major source of work ethics (Murtaza et al., 2016). By developing a solid appreciation of other religions, researchers and managers can better understand the work ethics associated with those religions.

Western ethic researchers, generally, have focused on Weber's (2013) Protestant work ethic (PWE, e.g., Giorgi & Marsh, 1990; Luna-Arocas & Tang, 2004; Hassall et al., 2005; Cokley et al., 2007). It would be rational to think that the PWE and other religion-based work ethics should inherently be dissimilar (Rawwas et al. 2018) as different religions are practiced in the world. Therefore, it would be logical to think that the PWE or any other religion-based work ethic could not be considered a global phenomenon (e.g. Niles, 1999; Arslan, 2001). Different religion-based work ethics would exist in the world, originating from the religion being practiced in any given specific location.

Islam is the second-largest religion of the world, after Christianity (Maoz & Henderson, 2013; Minhat & Dzolkarnaini, 2016). Over one-fifth of the total population of the world follows the tenets of Islam (Johnson & Grim, 2013). These facts make the religion of Islam a natural contender to be investigated more closely for its work ethic. As a result, IWE is the work ethic that caught scholars' attention (e.g. Ali, 1988). It would be logical and valuable for the organizations to study and understand IWE in those parts of the world where Islam is an accepted religion of the majority of people. So, it is clearly relevant to study IWE in the context of the Islamic Republic of Pakistan, a country which is the home of over 200 million Muslims.

Teachings of Islam may be placed into two ethical categories (Abuznaid, 2009). The first category is intended for Allah, the Almighty alone. The second category urges followers to build a pleasant relationship with fellow human beings and work with full sincerity and devotion to their employer (Ali, 1992; Javed et al., 2019). Islam has guided its followers in all aspects of human life (Rice, 1999) and emphasized specific actions of individuals to be performed according to the will of Allah, the Creator (Javed et al., 2019). Islamic teachings may potentially shape the thoughts and actions of their followers in society and the workplace. It was, then, logical to think that Islam should have guided its followers toward an Islamic work ethic as well. Various scholars have therefore focused their attention on exploring the Islamic perspective of the work ethic (e.g. Ali, 1988; Rice, 1999; Yousef, 2001).

Researchers have investigated various dimensions of IWE (Murtaza et al., 2016). Various models have been proposed to study the relationship between IWE and workplace-related job outcomes such as job satisfaction, turnover intentions, job involvement, organizational commitment, and organizational citizenship behavior (e.g., Yousef, 2001; Khan et al., 2015; Moayedi, 2009; Rokhman, 2010; Haroon et al., 2012; Alhyasat, 2012; Mursaleen et al., 2015). Some researchers confirmed the relationship between IWE and rewards, innovation capability, intrinsic motivation and job performance (Ahmad, 2011; Kumar & Che Rose, 2010; Hayati & Caniago, 2012).

Unlike PWE, IWE stressed more on intentions rather than results (Yousef, 2000b). IWE, as described by Yousef (2001), is a belief system that derived its origin from the Qur'an, a book believed by Muslims as the word of Allah, the Almighty, that was revealed to the Holy Prophet Muhammad (May Allah have peace be upon Him and His Family), and the Sunnah, the authentic and recorded sayings, traditions, and practices of the Holy Prophet Muhammad (May Allah have peace be upon Him and His Family).

As stated below, scholars have explored IWE in various interesting dimensions. Yousef (2000b) investigated the mediating role of organizational commitment between IWE and attitudes of the workforce toward change in organization. In another study, Yousef (2001) explored the moderating role of IWE in the relationships between job satisfaction and organizational commitment. Ali and Al-Owaihan (2008) explored IWE in the context of political, cultural and religious perspectives related to organizations and management. Later on, Uygur (2009) studied IWE and the behavior of Turkish entrepreneurs in the workplace. The role of IWE as a mediator between trust development and contributor of knowledge sharing was investigated by Mursaleen and colleagues (2015).

Several of the below-mentioned studies explored the relationship between IWE and its impact on workplace-related outcomes. For example, Moayedi (2009) confirmed that IWE was very strongly correlated with organizational commitment. Rokhman (2010) confirmed positive effects of IWE on both organizational commitment and job satisfaction, but with no significant effect on job turnover intentions. Haroon and colleagues (2012) studied the link between IWE and employee satisfaction in Pakistan and declared in favor of a robust relationship between these variables. A study, conducted in the context of Jordan, verified the effect of IWE on organizational citizenship behavior (Alhyasat, 2012). Marri and colleagues (2012) explored the impact of IWE on employee organizational commitment and job satisfaction in the context of Pakistan and found a strong positive relationship between these variables. Similarly, Kumar and Che Rose (2012) evidenced a significant impact of IWE on the motivation of employees toward inclination of knowledge sharing in Malaysian public sector organizations. Khan and colleagues (2015) tested the main effects of IWE and perceived organizational justice on turnover intentions, job satisfaction, and job involvement (Khan et al., 2015). Another study explored the impact of IWE on organizational citizenship and knowledge- sharing to find that IWE had a positive effect on the study variables (Murtaza et al., 2016) among employees of the public sector universities in Pakistan. A recent study conducted by Javed and colleagues (2019) confirmed that abusive supervision was positively related to deviant workplace behavior and the relationship was moderated by IWE. It is notable that many studies have indicated a positive contribution of IWE towards the job-related outcomes (e.g. Moayedi, 2009; Rokhman, 2010; Haroon et al., 2012).

It would be rational to relate and explain the above-mentioned discussion with the teachings of Islam, which all followers are obligated to practice. Also, these arguments may be supported by quoting the verses from the Holy Qur'an and the traditions of the Holy Prophet Muhammad (May Allah have peace be upon Him and His Family).The Holy Qur'an supports constructive behavior through creating discipline, acceptability, and respect for hierarchical order, by stating that "For all, there will be degrees by that which they did, and thy Lord is not unaware of that which they do" (Qur'an, 6:132). It has been stated in the Holy Qur'an that "…man can have nothing but what he strives for…" (Qur'an, 53:39). The Holy Prophet Muhammad (May Allah have peace be upon Him and His Family) is reported to have said, "Nobody has ever eaten a better meal than that which one has earned by working with one's own hands. As it is already stated above, the Prophet of Allah, David (Peace be upon Him & His Family) used to eat from the earnings of his manual labor" (Sahih Al-Bukhari, Hadith No. 2072). Some ethical principles that may directly be drawn from the Holy Qur'an and the traditions of the Holy Prophet Muhammad (May Allah has peace be upon Him and His Family) are work quality, knowledge-seeking, satisfying trust, and workplace requirement, giving full quantity and weight (Rice, 1999). These principles could be linked with the good conduct of the followers in the workplace. Believers of this philosophy will bring good for themselves as well as for their organization and society (Murtaza et al., 2016; Ahmad, 2011).

As mentioned earlier, the Holy Qur'an commanded believers into "enjoining what is right and forbidding what is wrong" (e.g. Qur'an, 3:104, 3:110 & 3:114). Also, one may relate an authentic and relevant saying of the Holy Prophet Muhammad (May Allah have peace be upon Him and His Family) that clearly instructed believers to express their proactive voice behavior. Abu Sa'id stated that he heard the Messenger of Allah (May Allah have peace be upon Him and His Family) as saying: "He who amongst you sees something abominable should modify it with the help of his hand, and if he has not strength enough to do it, then he should do it with his tongue, and if he has not strength enough to do it, (even) then he should (abhor it) from his heart, and that is the least of faith" (Sahih Muslim, Hadith No. 49a). These are the three levels of dealing with the act of evil, described by the Holy Prophet Muhammad (May Allah have peace be upon Him and His Family) mentioned here. The same concept may also be supported by some more traditions of the Holy Prophet Muhammad (May Allah have peace be upon Him and His Family). The Holy Prophet Muhammad (May Allah have peace be upon Him and His Family) has been reported to have said, "By Him in Whose Hand my life is, you either enjoin good and forbid evil, or Allah will certainly soon send His punishment to you. Then you will make supplication and it will not be accepted" (At-Tirmidhi, Hadith No.193). Another tradition narrated that 'Ayshah (May Allah be pleased with Her) said, "I heard the Messenger of Allah (Peace be upon Him and His Family) say, 'enjoin what is good and forbid what is evil before you call and you are not answered" (Sunan Ibn Majah, Hadith No. 4004). Keeping these religious teachings in view, this study investigates whether employees with a strong belief in Islamic teachings, reflected by their work ethis (IWE), show any concern about harmful activities at their workplace.

Some research has highlighted the individual personality differences and demographic characteristics as predictors of the voice behavior in the workplace (e.g., LePine & Van Dyne, 2001; Crant, 2003). Due to these personality differences, one might state that some individuals would be more prone to display voice behavior in the workplace than others, due to their unique background and characteristics.

Workplace voice behavior has been a much-debated research area (Brinsfield et al., 2009). Many researchers have focused on antecedents of the voice behavior in organizations (LePine & Van Dyne, 1998; Premeaux & Bedeian, 2003; Fuller et al., 2006; Detert & Burris, 2007; Thomas et al., 2010). LePine & Van Dyne, (1998) explored various personality differences of employees (e.g., self-esteem) as predictors of pro-social and informal voice behavior. Later, LePine and Van Dyne (2001) proposed extraversion personality characteristics as a predictor of voice behavior. Two independent studies proposed conscientiousness as a predictor of voice behavior (LePine & Van Dyne, 2001; Thomas, et al., 2010). A different personality trait, i.e. proactive personality, was identified by Parker and Collins (2010) as a predictor of workplace voice behavior. Detert and Burris (2007) confirmed that openness in leadership style and behavior correlated with the voice behavior of employees. Thus, the proactive voice behavior demonstrated by employees might be considered by them as an opportunity to avoid a potential threat or to improve the current state of affairs in an organization.

Keeping in view the Islamic teachings discussed above, it would be justified to relate employee voice behavior with their IWE in the workplace. The PVB is a type of workplace-related behavior demonstrated by employees to express their distress about practices, incidents, or behaviors that could damage interests of the organization (Bijleveld & Baalbergen, 2017). Therefore, it may be argued that IWE would be positively related to the voice behavior of employees.

Hypothesis 1: Islamic work ethics are significantly and positively related to prohibitive voice behavior of employees.

The conceptual model of the study is shown in Figure 3.

Figure 3

Conceptual Model of Study 3

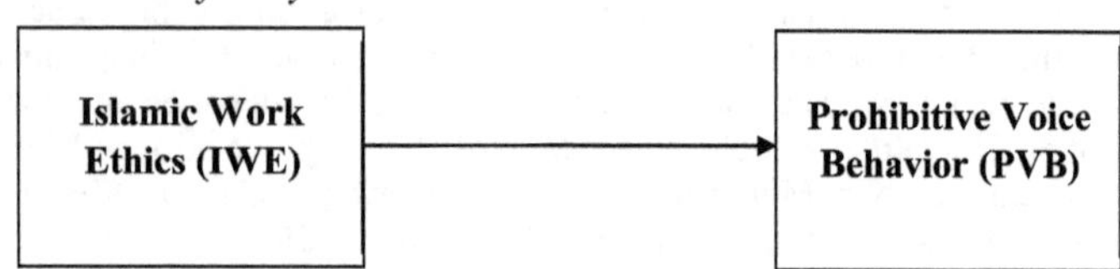

The proposed hypothesis is tested in the next chapter.

2.5   Chapter Summary

This chapter analyzed the related literature in three different aspects. In the first aspect of the review, IWE and WD related literature were reviewed that led to an interesting finding. Research that had examined the influence of IWE on employees' perceived abusive supervision, while considering WD, was scarce and limited in scope. Earlier studies had not investigated the said relationship. While this analysis pointed toward a relationship between these variables, after a thorough review, it was argued that IWE plays its role in reducing employees' perceived abusive supervision. So, it was also proposed that IWE and WD play their role in predicting employees' perceived abusive supervision.

In the second aspect of the review, IWE and WD related literature was reviewed again, but in a different way. It suggested that a link existed between IWE and WD. Previous research that had examined this relationship did not consider the moderation of employees' perceived abusive supervision between IWE & WD. Moreover, previous studies had not tested the mediating role performed by employees' hostility regarding the said relationship. So, it was proposed that employee's hostility started taking effect after a certain amount of employees' perceived abusive supervision. Consequently, it appeared that IWE was to impact WD. In addition, the proposed relationship was to be moderated by employees' perceived abusive supervision and mediated by their hostility.

In the third aspect of the review, the IWE and PVB related literature was explored for the last study that revealed some very interesting research gaps. The analysis of the related studies pointed toward a clear relationship between IWE and PVB. It was surprisingly missing in the literature. Therefore, after a thorough review of the literature, it was suggested that IWE was to impact PVB of employees and the relationship was proposed to be strong and positive.

The literature review conducted in the above-stated three different dimensions pushed the argument ahead and directed toward the development of three theorized models and relevant hypotheses.

The next chapter, Chapter 3, discusses the research methods adopted to test the proposed research models and hypotheses, along with the instruments used to measure the variables.

Chapter 3

Research Methodology and Analysis

3.1 Introduction

In the preceding chapter, a thorough review of literature was conducted that theorized relationships among studied variables. In the last part of each section of this chapter, hypothetical models and related hypotheses of each study were outlined. These hypothesized relationships are tested in this chapter.

This chapter begins by discussing design of the research including sampling details, characteristics of the sample, methods used to collect data, and ethical considerations. The chapter then unfolds to talk about the measures and items employed in each study. The final part of the chapter discusses reliability and validity issues. Then CFA is performed. The items confirmed on the basis of the CFA are then investigated for reliability of scale by means of analyzing Cronbach alpha. Afterward, regression analyses, using well-known computer software were run to investigate the suggested hypotheses of each study, along with the results obtained from the regression analyses are presented in tables. Finally, toward the end of each study, the results obtained are discussed.

3.2 Study 1: Islamic Work Ethics and Workplace Deviance: Antecedents of Abusive Supervision

3.2.1 Sample and Procedures

The data were collected through self-administered surveys, written in English and coded for proper matching. The population of the study is all full-time managers or supervisors and employees working in the private sector organizations, operating in or around the city of Lahore, Pakistan. The rationale behind collecting data from diverse sectors is to increase the generalizability of the study and not to limit the study to only one sector or industry.

The surveys were completed by 250 employees of diverse organizations operating in the private. The data collection was performed in and around Lahore, which is the capital of the largest province, the Punjab, and the second-largest city in the country. Surveys were distributed with a cover letter that explained the rationale of the research and guaranteed the secrecy and anonymity of respondents.

The respondents were full-time employees belonging to diverse types of organizations specializing in manufacturing, engineering, banking and transportation, and information technology. One hundred eighty-nine (189) completed surveys were received. Only those surveys were included in the analysis where responses received were from one supervisor and at least two or more matching subordinates working under the same supervisor. The recorded response rate (76%) is in accordance with studies performed in a similar context (e.g., Raja et al., 2004; Abbas et al., 2014). Results revealed by demographics confirmed that a large percentage (87%) of the respondents were males.

Common method bias was avoided by collecting data in two, at least one month apart, waves (Podsakoff et al., 2003). At wave one, supervisors' and their selected employees' responses were recorded. At wave two, the same set of subordinates responded to items related to job outcome.

3.2.2 Measures

The Likert-type scale, ranging from 1=strongly disagree to 5=strongly agree, was employed for the items. Employee performance, evaluated by supervisors, was rated from unacceptable to outstanding and very ineffective to very effective.

3.2.2.1 Islamic Work Ethics (IWE)

IWE was measured at wave 1, using a scale that has 17 items, developed by Ali (1988). Item 9 was reverse coded. Cronbach's alpha for the scale was 0.90. The items used are given below:

1. Laziness is a vice (defect).

2. Dedication to work is a virtue (good behavior).

3. Good work benefits both one's self and others.

4. Justice and generosity in the workplace are necessary conditions for society's welfare.

5. Producing more than enough to meet one's personal needs contributes to the prosperity of society as a whole.

6. One should carry work out to the best of one's ability.

7. Work is not an end in itself but a means to foster personal growth and social relations.

8. Life has no meaning without work.

9. More leisure time is good for society. (Reverse coded)

10. Human relations in organizations should be emphasized and encouraged.

11. Work enables man to control nature.

12. Creative work is a source of happiness and accomplishment.

13. Any man who works is more likely to get ahead in life.

14. Work gives one the chance to be independent.

15. A successful man is the one who meets deadlines at work.

16. One should constantly work hard to meet responsibilities.

17. The value of work is derived from the accompanying intentions rather than the results.

3.2.2.2 Workplace Deviance

Deviance of employees in the workplace was measured using a nineteen-item scale (Bennett & Robinson, 2000). Data to measure workplace deviance were collected at wave 1. Cranach's alpha for the scale was 0.93. The following items were used:

1. I make fun of someone at work.

2. I say something hurtful/painful to someone at work.

3. I make an ethnic, religious, or racial remark at work.

4. I curse at someone at work.

5. I play a mean prank (joke) on someone at work.

6. I act rudely towards someone at work.

7. I publicly embarrass someone at work.

8. I take property from work without permission.

9. I spend too much time fantasizing or daydreaming instead of working.

10. I falsify a receipt to get reimbursed for more money than I spent on business expenses.

11. I take an additional or longer break than is acceptable at my workplace.

12.   I come in late to work without permission.

13.   I litter (throw garbage in) my work environment.

14.   I neglect to follow my supervisor's instructions.

15.   I intentionally work slower than I could have worked.

16.   I discuss confidential company information with an unauthorized person.

17.   I use an illegal drug or consumed alcohol on the job.

18.   I put little effort into my work.

19.   I drag out (delay) work in order to get overtime.

3.2.2.3 Employee Perceived Abusive Supervision

A scale, consisting of fifteen items, developed by Tepper (2000) was applied to measure perceived supervisory abusive. Cronbach's alpha for the scale was 0.92. The following items were used:

1.   My supervisor ridicules me.

2.   My supervisor tells me my thoughts or feelings are stupid.

3.   My supervisor gives me the silent treatment.

4.   My supervisor puts me down in front of others.

5.   My supervisor invades my privacy.

6.   My supervisor reminds me of my past mistakes and failures.

7.   My supervisor doesn't give me credit for jobs requiring a lot of effort.

8.   My supervisor blames me for his or her own mistakes.

9.   My supervisor breaks promises he or she makes.

10.   My supervisor expresses anger at me when he or she is mad for another reason.

11.   My supervisor makes negative comments about me to others.

12.   My supervisor is rude to me.

13.   My supervisor does not allow me to interact with my coworkers.

14.   My supervisor tells me I am incompetent.

15.   My supervisor lies to me.

3.2.2.4 Control Variables

The gender of supervisor and subordinates was controlled for, because males and females report workplace victimization differently (Nixon, 2009). Gender similarity was controlled for, as males were typically persecuted by other males and often by their supervisors, while females might be victimized by both genders (Cortina et al., 2002; Salin, 2003; Zapf et al., 2003). Experience under existing supervisor, supervisor-rated employee performance and hierarchy level of the employee were also controlled for, as previous studies indicated a strong relationship between some demographic variables and perceived supervisory abuse (Wu & Hu, 2013).

Therefore, controlled-for variables included the following: supervisor's gender, gender similarity between supervisor and subordinate, work experience under the current supervisor, supervisor-rated employee performance, and hierarchical level of a subordinate in the organization.

3.2.3 Results

The confirmatory factor analysis (CFA) was conducted to evaluate factor configuration along with the discriminant validity of observed scales - IWE, WD, perceived abusive supervision and subordinate performance. AMOS, with maximum likelihood estimation, was employed to assess model-fitness (Arbuckle & Wothke, 1999). Afterward, the hypotheses were tested.

3.2.3.1 Confirmatory Factor Analysis (CFA)

The validity, both convergent and discriminant, of the collected data was established using the CFA. Convergent validity was verified by the factor-loading score of each item on its particular construct (Parasuraman et al., 2002; Park et al., 2006). Items with loading lower than 0.40 were excluded (Comrey, 1978).

For a scale having numerous items, inflated measurement errors may arise (Judge et al., 2002). The potential issue was addressed by applying the parceling technique. Constructs with numerous items were grouped into parcels (Smith & Webster, 2017).

The heterogeneous assignment of items (Cole et al., 2016) was used for IWE and WD scales which allowed varying numbers of items in parcels. The IWE scale was divided into a total of four parcels. Due to low factor loadings, four items were excluded from the analysis. The WD scale was bundled into five parcels. The perceived abusive supervision scale was packed into five parcels.

To evaluate the model fitness in CFA, the Chi-Square Statistic, Root Mean Square Error of Approximation (RMSEA; acceptable fit: 0.05 – 0.08), the Standardized Root Mean Square Residual (SRMR; acceptable fit: 0.05 – 0.10, good fit: 0 – 0.08), the Comparative Fit Index (CFI; acceptable fit: 0.90– 0.97, good fit: 0.97–1) and the Tucker-Lewis Index (TLI; acceptable fit: greater than 0.90; Bentler & Bonett, 1980; Bentler, 1990; Hu & Bentler, 1999; Schermelleh-Engel et al., 2003; Marsh et al., 2004; Chen et al., 2008) were used.

Table 3.2.1

CFA Measurement Models

Model	Factors	CMIN/df	RMSEA	CFI	RMR	TLI
1	Proposed four factors	296.66/146 = 2.03	0.07	0.93	0.05	0.92
2	One factor (All factors combined)	1614.45/155 = 10.42	0.22	0.36	0.19	0.29

As shown in the Model 1 Table 3.2.1, indices indicated a good fit. The proposed four-factor model, vis-à-vis the one-factor model, indicated a better fit and confirmed the discriminant validity of all four scales. Based on low factor loading, four items of the IWE scale were removed (Kline, 2015). That improved the model fitness. For Model 1, all fit statistics were satisfactory (CMIN/df = 2.0, $p < 0.10$, CFI = 0.93, RMSEA = 0.07, RMR = 0.05, TLI = 0.92). The results confirmed the convergent and discriminant validity of the study variables. Thus, CFA results indicated in the Table 3.2.1 show that the data were suitable for hypotheses testing.

3.2.3.2 Demographic Information, Descriptive Statistics, Scales of Reliability and Correlation Results

The demographic information about the controlled for variables is given in the below given Table 3.2.2.

Table 3.2.2

Demographic Information

Variable		Frequency	Percentage
Supervisor's Gender	Male	165	87.3
	Female	24	12.7
Subordinate's Gender	Male	164	86.8
	Female	25	13.2
Supervisor-Subordinate Gender Similarity	Gender Mismatch	29	15.3
	Gender Match	160	84.7
Employee's Experience Under Current Supervisor	Less than a year	77	40.7
	1-2 years	62	32.8
	3-5 years	37	19.6
	6-10 years	11	5.8
	More than 10 years	2	1.1
Subordinate's Hierarchy	Entry level	70	37.0
	Middle level	100	52.9
	Senior level	19	10.1
Note: N = 189			

The mean, standard deviation, minimum and maximum values of the controlled for and observed variables are given in the following Table 3.2.3.

Table 3.2.3

Descriptive Statistics

Variable	Mean	Standard Deviation	Minimum	Maximum
Supervisor's Gender	1.13	0.33	1	2
Subordinate's Gender	0.85	0.36	0	1
Supervisor-Subordinate Gender Similarity	1.94	0.97	1	5
Employee's Experience Under Current Supervisor	1.13	0.34	1	2
Subordinate's Hierarchy	1.73	0.63	1	3
Islamic Work Ethics	3.73	0.57	2.00	5.00
Workplace Deviance	2.36	0.79	1.00	4.33
Perceived Abusive Supervision	2.65	0.76	1.00	4.73
Supervisor-rated Subordinate Performance	3.54	0.77	1.50	5.00
Note N = 189				

Cronbach's alpha reliability values of the observed variables and correlations between controlled for variables and the observed variables are given in the following Tables 3.2.4 and 3.2.5 respectively.

Table 3.2.4

Cronbach's Alpha Reliability

Sr. No.	Constructs	No. of Items	Cronbach's Alpha Value
1.	Islamic Work Ethics	17	0.90
2.	Workplace Deviance	19	0.93
3.	Abusive Supervision	15	0.92
4.	Supervisor-rated Subordinate Performance	4	0.80
Note N = 189			

Table 3.2.5

Correlations

	1	2	3	4	5	6	7	8	9
Islamic Work Ethic	-								
Workplace Deviance	-0.29**	-							
Perceived Abusive Supervision	-0.29**	0.44**							
Supervisor-rated Subordinate Performance	0.32**	-0.09	-0.03						
Supervisor's gender (a)	0.15*	-0.19**	-0.12	0.09					
Supervisor–subordinate gender similarity (b)	-0.07	0.16*	0.07	-0.10	-0.46**				
Experience under current supervisor (c)	-0.03	-0.07	-0.17*	-0.05	0.06	-0.03			
Subordinate's gender (d)	0.15*	-0.22**	-0.15*	0.12	0.32**	-0.48**	0.03		
Subordinate's hierarchical level (e)	0.06	-0.18*	-0.02	0.07	0.04	-0.18*	0.38**	-0.01	-

Notes: N = 189. * p < 0.05, ** p < 0.01,
    (a) Supervisor's gender codes: 1 = Male, 2 = Female,
    (b) Supervisor–subordinate gender similarity codes: 0=Mismatch, 1=Match,
       For subordinate-supervisor same gender=1, different genders=0,
    (c) Experience with current supervisor coded: 1 = less than 1 year,
       2 = 1–2 years, 3 = 3–5 years, 4 = 6–10 years, 5 = more than 10 years,
    (d) Subordinate's gender coded: 1=Male, 2=Female,
    (e) Subordinate's hierarchical level coded: 1=Entry level, 2=Middle level,
       3=Senior level

According to the results of Table 3.2.5, IWE was negatively correlated with workplace deviance (r = -0.29, p < 0.01). Also, WD was positively related to employees' perceived abusive behavior (r = 0.44, p < 0.01). These results were in accordance with the proposed model and encouraged continuing and testing the hypotheses.

The gender of a subordinate showed a negative relation with the perceived supervisory abusive (r = -0.15, p < 0.01), suggesting that female workers reported lower perceived abusive supervision than males. Also, experience under the current supervisor and perceived abusive supervision were negatively linked (r = -0.17, p < 0.05), implying that employees who spent a long time with supervisors perceived lower levels of abuse.

3.2.4 Hypotheses Testing

Hypotheses test results are given below in Tables 3.2.6, 3.2.7 and 3.2.8. These results pertain to the impact of IWE on WD and the direct and indirect effects of WD and employees' supervisor-reported performance on their perceived victimization shown by supervisors.

Controlled variables were entered in Model 1. Results indicate that WD is negatively but significantly linked with the gender of the supervisor and subordinate. However, it is also negatively but very significantly linked with the subordinate's hierarchical level.

Table 3.2.6

Regression Results

Variable	Workplace Deviance		Perceived Abusive Supervision		
	Model 1	Model 2	Model 3	Model 4	Model 5
Supervisor's Gender	-0.33*	-0.26	-0.20	-0.11	-0.01
Supervisor–subordinate Gender Similarity	-0.08	-0.04	-0.07	-0.03	-0.01
Experience Under Current Supervisor	0.01	0.00	-0.14*	-0.15	-0.15**
Subordinate's Gender	-0.44*	-0.38*	-0.30	-0.22	-0.08
Subordinate's Hierarchical Level	-0.23**	-0.21**	0.05	0.07	0.15*
Supervisor-rated Subordinate Performance	-0.05	0.03	-0.02	0.07	0.06
Subordinate's Islamic Work Ethics	-	-0.35**	-	-0.41***	-0.27**
Subordinate Workplace Deviance	-	-	-	-	0.38***
R^2	0.10	0.15	0.06	0.14	0.27

Notes: $N = 189$; * $p < 0.05$, **$p < 0.01$, *** $p < 0.001$

To test these hypotheses, multiple linear regressions were run. The effects of control variables on WD are shown in Model 1, Table 3.2.6.

The effects of IWE and all control variables are shown in Model 2 in Table 3.2.6. These results demonstrate a significant and negative relationship between IWE and WD (β = -0.35, $p < 0.01$). This indicates that employees possessing strong IWE are less inclined toward WD. The results empirically support hypothesis 1.

Model 3 in Table 3.2.6 shows the effects of control variables on subordinate perceived abusive supervision. These results specify that employees' experience under the current supervisor is negatively but strongly associated with employees' perception of abusive supervisory behavior (β = -0.14, p < 0.01).

Model 4 presented in Table 3.2.6, indicates the effects of the controlled-for variables and IWE on employees' perceived abusive supervision. The results of Model 4 and Model 5, given in Table 3.2.6, show a negative and very significant relationship between IWE and subordinate perceived abusive supervisory behavior (β = -0.41, p < 0.01). The results of Model 5, given in Table 3.2.6, show a very highly significant and positive relationship between WD and perceived abusive supervision (β = 0.38, p < 0.001). These results support hypothesis 2.

Hypothesis 3 is tested by making use of the SPSS PROCESS, proposed by Hayes and Preacher (2014), by adopting the mediation approach. Table 3.2.7 and Table 3.2.8 sum up the test results of the conditional effect of IWE on the perceptions of supervisory abuse through WD of subordinates.

Table 3.2.7

Mediation Results

Variable	Employee deviant workplace behavior	Subordinate perceived abusive supervision
	Model 6	**Model 7**
Supervisor's gender	-0.26	-0.01
Supervisor – subordinate gender similarity	-0.04	-0.01
Experience under present supervisor	0.00	-0.15*
Subordinate's gender	-0.38*	-0.08
Hierarchical level of subordinate	-0.21**	0.15
Supervisor-rated subordinate performance	0.03	0.06
Islamic work ethics	-0.35***	-0.27***
Workplace deviance	-	0.38***
R^2	0.15	0.26

Notes: N=189; * p < 0.05, ** p < 0.01, *** p < 0.001

Model 6 in Table 3.2.7 indicates that the relationship between IWE and WD is negative and highly significant (β = - 0.35, p < 0.001). Model 7 in Table 3.2.7 indicates that the effect of deviant behavior on employees' perceived abusive supervisory behavior is significant and positive (β = 0.38, p < 0.001).

Table 3.2.8

Mediation Results

Effect of IWE on abusive behavior	Effect	Boot SE	95% Bias-Corrected Confidence Interval	
			Lower	Upper
Total-effect	-0.40***	0.10	-0.60	-0.21
Direct-effect	-0.27***	0.09	-0.46	-0.09
Indirect-effect	-0.13	0.05	-0.26	-0.05
Partially standardized effect	-0.17	0.07	-0.34	-0.06
Completely standardized indirect effect	-0.09	0.04	-0.18	-0.03
Ratio of indirect to the total effect	0.32	0.17	0.10	0.72
Ratio of indirect to direct effect	0.48	8.6	0.10	2.36

Notes: N=189; *p<.05, **p<.01, ***p<.001

Table 3.2.8 indicates measured values of the total effect, direct effect, indirect effect, partially standardized, completely standardized indirect, the ratio of indirect-to-total effect, and the ratio of indirect-to-direct effect.

The indirect effect of IWE on perceived supervisory abuse through WD is reported in Table 3.2.8. The confidence intervals for this indirect effect do not include zero (β = -0.13, 95% CI [-0.26, 0.05]). Thus, it may be deduced that there is a significant negative indirect effect (i.e. mediation) of IWE on perceived supervisory abuse in the presence of WD. These results support hypothesis 3.

3.2.5 Discussion

The study contributes to the literature by verifying that IWE plays significant part in reducing employees' perceived abusive supervision through WD. These results confirm that employees with higher IWE are less deviant. Also, the employees who show low WD face lower supervisory abuse. Also, when subordinates demonstrate WD, they invite trouble by presenting supervisors with a soft target of supervisory abuse. This study aligns with the research that explores employee-specific behaviors and the antecedents of abusive supervision (e.g., Aquino & Bradfield, 2000; Tepper et al., 2006; Tepper et al., 2011; Hogler et al., 2013; Neves, 2014). It adds to the literature by showing IWE and WD as two new antecedents of perceived abusive supervision in an important but relatively less explored context of Pakistan.

Additionally, this study responds to the recent call for more research by finding evidence in support of a set of two additional subordinate-specific antecedents of employees' perceived supervisory abuse (Hogler et al., 2013; Khan et al., 2017).

3.3 Study 2: Islamic Work Ethics and Workplace Deviance: Moderated by Abusive Supervision and Mediated by Employee Hostility

3.3.1 Sample and Procedures

The population of the study is all full-time managers or supervisors and employees working in the private sector organizations, operating in or around the city of Lahore, Pakistan. The rationale behind collecting data from diverse sectors is to increase the generalizability of the study and not to limit the study to only one sector or industry.

The data were collected through a set of self-administered, written in English and coded for proper matching, questionnaires. The data collection was performed in and around Lahore, which is the capital of the largest province, the Punjab, and the second-largest city of Pakistan. The respondents were full-time employees of organizations specializing in manufacturing, engineering, transportation, banking, and information technology in the private sector of Pakistan.

A cover letter that stated the purpose of the study and guaranteed respondents' secrecy and anonymity was distributed with the survey questionnaires.

The total number of surveys distributed was 250. Out of which, 189 completed surveys were returned. Only those surveys were included in the analysis where responses received were from one supervisor and at least two or more matching subordinates working under the same supervisor. The response rate was about 76% which is in line with other research carried by Raja and colleagues (2004) and Abbas et al. (2014) in a similar regional perspective. Results revealed by demographics confirmed that a large percentage (87%) of the respondents were males.

Common method bias (Podsakoff et al., 2003) was avoided by collecting data in two waves. These waves were at least one month apart.

At wave one, employees were requested to respond to the items pertaining to Islamic work ethics (IWE), abusive supervision, hostility, generalized self-efficacy (GSE) and demographics (e.g., age, gender, experience under the current supervisor and total professional experience). After one month, at wave two, the same set of subordinates was requested to respond to items related to job outcomes (e.g., deviant workplace behavior).

3.3.2 Measures

The five-point Likert-type scale, ranging from 1=strongly disagree to 5=strongly agree, was employed for every item.

The detail of the measures employed in the study is given below.

3.3.2.1 Islamic Work Ethics (IWE)

A17-item scale was used to measure IWE (Ali, 1988). IWE was measured in wave 1. Item 9 was reverse coded. Cronbach's alpha for the scale was 0.90. The following items were used.

1. Laziness is a vice (defect).

2. Dedication to work is a virtue (good behavior).

3. Good work benefits both one's self and others.

4. Justice and generosity in the workplace are necessary conditions for society's welfare.

5. Producing more than enough to meet one's personal needs contributes to the prosperity of society as a whole.

6. One should carry work out to the best of one's ability.

7. Work is not an end in itself but a means to foster personal growth and social relations.

8. Life has no meaning without work.

9. More leisure time is good for society. (Reverse coded)

10. Human relations in organizations should be emphasized and encouraged.

11. Work enables man to control nature.

12. Creative work is a source of happiness and accomplishment.

13. Any man who works is more likely to get ahead in life.

14. Work gives one the chance to be independent.

15. A successful man is the one who meets deadlines at work.

16. One should constantly work hard to meet responsibilities.

17. The value of work is derived from the accompanying intentions rather than the results.

3.3.2.2 Employees' Perceived Abusive Supervision

Data to measure abusive supervision were collected in wave 1. Employees' perceived abusive supervision was measured through the 15-item scale introduced by Tepper (2000). Cronbach's alpha for the scale was 0.92. The following items were used:

1. My supervisor ridicules me.

2. My supervisor tells me my thoughts or feelings are stupid.

3. My supervisor gives me the silent treatment.

4. My supervisor puts me down in front of others.

5. My supervisor invades my privacy.

6. My supervisor reminds me of my past mistakes and failures.

7. My supervisor doesn't give me credit for jobs requiring a lot of effort.

8. My supervisor blames me for his or her own mistakes.

9. My supervisor breaks promises he or she makes.

10. My supervisor expresses anger at me when he or she is mad for another reason.

11. My supervisor makes negative comments about me to others.

12. My supervisor is rude to me.

13. My supervisor does not allow me to interact with my coworkers.

14. My supervisor tells me I am incompetent.

15. My supervisor lies to me.

3.3.2.3 Workplace Deviance

Deviance of employees in the workplace was measured using a nineteen-item scale (Bennett & Robinson, 2000). Data to measure workplace deviance was collected at wave 1. Cronbach's alpha for the scale was 0.93. The following items were used:

1. I make fun of someone at work.

2. I say something hurtful/painful to someone at work.

3. I make an ethnic, religious, or racial remark at work.

4. I curse at someone at work.

5. I play a mean prank (joke) on someone at work.

6. I act rudely towards someone at work.

7. I publicly embarrass someone at work.

8. I take property from work without permission.

9. I spend too much time fantasizing or daydreaming instead of working.

10. I falsify a receipt to get reimbursed for more money than I spent on business expenses.

11. I take an additional or longer break than is acceptable at my workplace.

12. I come in late to work without permission.

13. I litter (throw garbage in) my work environment.

14.   I neglect to follow my supervisor's instructions.

15.   I intentionally work slower than I could have worked.

16.   I discuss confidential company information with an unauthorized person.

17.   I use an illegal drug or consumed alcohol on the job.

18.   I put little effort into my work.

19.   I drag out (delay) work in order to get overtime.

3.3.2.4 Employee Hostility

Employee Hostility was measured with a scale that has eight items. The scale used in the study was developed by Buss and Perry (1992). Data to measure the hostile behavior of employees were collected in wave 1. Cronbach's alpha for the scale was 0.80. The following items were used:

1.   I am sometimes eaten up with (controlled by) jealousy.

2.   At times I feel I have gotten a raw deal (unfair treatment) out of life.

3.   Other people always seem to get the breaks (opportunities).

4.   I wonder why sometimes I feel so bitter about things.

5.   I know that "friends/colleagues" talk about me behind my back.

6.   I am suspicious of overly friendly strangers.

7.   I sometimes feel that people are laughing at me behind my back.

8.   When people are especially (more than ever) nice, I wonder what they want.

3.3.2.5 Control Variables

Some variables, which are demographic in nature, may affect the proposed relationships. Previous research has suggested that employee age, gender, job experience and employee experience under current supervisor may explain negative reactions to their perceived supervisor's abusive behavior (Judge et al., 2000; Aquino & Douglas, 2003; Aquino & Thau, 2009; Mayer et al., 2012). Therefore, these employee demographics were controlled for in the study.

To take changes in the competency level of employees into account, that might affect their predicted behavior, employees' GSE was also controlled for (Judge et al., 2000) and was measured using a scale adapted from the eight-item measure developed by Judge and colleagues (2000). Item number two, four, five and seven were reverse coded. Based on low factor loadings (Kline, 2015), four items of the GSE scale were removed. Cronbach's alpha for the scale was 0.70. The following were the items of the GSE scale:

1.   I am strong enough to overcome life's struggles.

2.   At root (basically), I am a weak person. (Reverse coded)

3.   I can handle the situations that life brings.

4.   I usually feel that I am an unsuccessful person. (Reverse coded)

5.   I often feel that there is nothing that I can do well. (Reverse coded)

6.   I feel competent to deal effectively with the real world.

7.   I often feel like a failure. (Reverse coded)

8.   I usually feel I can handle the typical problems that come up in life.

3.3.3 Results

The confirmatory factor analysis (CFA) was conducted to evaluate factor configuration along with the discriminant validity of all observed scales—IWE, employee perceived abusive supervision, WD and hostility. AMOS, with maximum likelihood estimation, was employed to assess model-fitness (Arbuckle & Wothke, 1999). Afterward, the hypotheses were tested.

3.3.3.1 Confirmatory Factor Analysis (CFA)

Confirmatory factor analysis (CFA) was performed to verify convergent as well as discriminant validity of the observed variables by confirming whether the data followed the assumption that all of the employed latent variables represented distinct constructs. Convergent validity of the variables was verified through the loading score of the factors of each item on the corresponding construct (Parasuraman et al., 2002; Park et al., 2006). The items that had a score of 0.40 or more were used in the analysis (Comrey, 1978).

While dealing with a scale comprising a large number of items to explain a specific construct, the issue of inflated measurement errors may arise (Judge et al., 2002). This issue would cause an unfavorable effect on the fitness of the model, and it can be addressed by applying the parceling technique (Smith & Webster, 2017). Following the same technique, constructs with numerous items were grouped into parcels.

For both IWE and deviant workplace behavior scales, the heterogeneous assignment of items (Cole et al., 2016) was used that allowed varying numbers of items in parcels. The 17-item Islamic work ethics scale was packed into a total of four parcels. Four items with low factor loadings were not included in the analysis. The 19-item deviant workplace behavior scale was packed into a total of five parcels. Similarly, the 15-item perceived abusive supervision scale was packed into a total of five parcels.

GSE was controlled for, along with the following demographic variables: age of the employee, gender, the experience of the employee under a current supervisor, and total experience of the employee (Mayer et al., 2012).

To evaluate the model fitness in CFA: Chi-Square Statistic, RMSEA with acceptable fit: 0.05 – 0.08, SRMR with acceptable fit: 0.05 – 0.10 & good fit: 0 – 0.08), CFI with acceptable fit: 0.90 – 0.97 & good fit: 0.97 – 1, and TLI with acceptable fit greater than 0.90 (Bentler & Bonett, 1980; Bentler, 1990; Hu & Bentler, 1999; Schermelleh-Engel et al., 2003; Marsh et al., 2004; Chen et al., 2008) were used.

Each item was constrained to load on the respective variable and the results show a reasonable full-model fit ($\chi2/df$ = 2.02; RMSEA = 0.07; SRMR = 0.06; CFI = 0.90; TLI = 0.90). All loadings of the items were significant. Thus, convergent validity of the used constructs was verified.

To establish constructs' discriminant validity, the CFA model of measurement was used. The complete hypothesized model of the study that included four factors of measurement was depicted as an improved fitness against all other substitute models. Thus, the discriminant validity of the hypothesized model was confirmed. The results confirmed the convergent as well as the discriminant validity of the study variables. Therefore, these CFA results showed that the data on hand were appropriate for hypotheses testing.

3.3.3.2 Demographic Information, Descriptive Statistics, Reliability and Correlation Results

Demographic information is shown in Table 3.3.1. The descriptive statistics of all controlled for and main variable are given in the Table 3.3.2.

The correlations between the control variables (GSE, employee age, gender, job experience and employee experience under current supervisor) with the main study variables are also given in Table 3.3.3. Employee age, job experience and experience of the employee under the current supervisor are in years. Cronbach's alpha reliability is stated in the Table 3.3.4.

Table 3.3.1

Demographic Information

Variable		Frequency	Percentage
Age	Less than 25 years	54	28.6
	25-30 years	86	45.5
	31-34 years	31	16.4
	35-40 years	12	6.3
	41-44 years	2	1.1
	45-50 years	1	0.5
	51-54 years	1	0.5
	55 years and above	2	1.1
Gender	Male	164	86.8
	Female	25	13.2
Employee Experience	Less than 5 years	144	76.2
	6-10 years	34	18.0
	11-15 years	8	4.2
	More than 15 years	3	1.6
Experience Under Current Supervisor	Less than a year	77	40.7
	1-2 years	62	32.8
	3-5 years	37	19.6
	6-10 years	11	5.8
	More than 10 years	2	1.1
Note. N = 189			

Table 3.3.2

Descriptive Statistics

Variable	Mean	Standard Deviation	Minimum	Maximum
Employee Age	26	5.18	1.00	8.00
Employee Gender	1.13	0.34	1.00	2.00
Employee Experience	1.31	0.63	1.00	4.00
Experience Under Current Supervisor	1.94	0.97	1.00	5.00
Generalized Self-Efficacy	3.60	0.69	1.50	5.00
Islamic Work Ethics	3.73	0.57	2.00	5.00
Abusive Supervision	2.65	0.76	1.00	4.73
Workplace Deviance	2.36	0.79	1.00	4.33
Hostility	3.23	0.62	1.25	5.00
Note: N = 189				

Table 3.3.3

Correlation Analysis

Variable	1	2	3	4	5	6	7	8
Employee Age	-							
Employee Gender	-0.12	-						
Employee Experience	0.64**	-0.07	-					
Experience Under Current Supervisor	0.31**	0.03	0.46**	-				
Generalized Self-Efficacy	0.14*	0.02	0.04	-0.01				
Islamic Work Ethics	0.09	0.15*	-0.03	-0.03	0.49**			
Abusive Supervision	-0.11	-0.15*	-0.19**	-0.17*	-0.17*	-0.29**		
Workplace Deviance	-0.09	-0.22**	0.02	-0.07	-0.26**	-0.29**	0.44**	
Hostility	-0.09	0.11	-0.10	-0.04	0.15*	0.16*	0.43**	0.18**

Notes: N = 189; Scale reliability coefficients are mentioned diagonally in parentheses; Age and experience in years; * p < .05. ** p < .01.

As per the tests of correlation, as predicted, IWE was negatively correlated with employees' workplace deviance ($\beta = -0.29$, p<0.01) and perceived abusive supervision ($\beta = -0.29$, p< 0.01). Moreover, subordinates' deviance was positively correlated with their perceived abusive supervision (r = 0.44, p<0.01). Furthermore, correlations between employee perceived abusive supervision and employee hostility ($\beta = 0.43$, p < 0.01) and between workplace deviance and employee hostility ($\beta = 0.18$, p < 0.01) were positive. These correlations are in line with the previous literature (e.g. Javed et al. 2019). Encouraged by these findings, as these were consistent with the hypothesized relationships, the proposed model was tested. The correlations of the main model and control variables are shown in Table 3.3.3.

Table 3.3.4

Cronbach's Alpha Reliability

Sr. No.	Constructs	No. of Items	Cronbach's Alpha
1.	Generalized Self-Efficacy	8	0.70
2.	Islamic Work Ethics	17	0.90
3.	Abusive Supervision	15	0.92
4.	Workplace Deviance	19	0.93
5.	Hostility	8	0.80

Cronbach's Alpha reliability values of all main variables: Generalized self-efficacy, Islamic work ethics, abusive supervision, workplace deviance and hostility, are given in the Table 3.3.4.

3.3.4 Hypotheses Testing

The regression results are shown in Tables 3.3.5 and 3.3.6. Model 1 in Table 3.3.5 shows the effect of all controlled-for variables on employee hostility. The results indicate that, with the exception of GSE ($\beta = 0.15$, $p < 0.05$), the effect of all other control variables on employee hostility is non-significant.

The relationship between IWE and employee hostility, while not explicitly hypothesized, was tested using multiple regressions in Model 2 Table 3.3.5. These results indicate an insignificant link between IWE and employee hostility. It means that workers with IWE are not hostile under normal conditions.

The Model 3 Table 3.3.5 shows the effects of all controlled-for variables on workplace deviance. The results indicate that, with the exception of GSE and employee gender, the effect of all other control variables on workplace deviance is non-significant. In contrast, the effect of GSE on workplace deviance is very significant but negative ($\beta = -0.28$, $p < 0.01$). The effect of employee gender on workplace deviance is also significant but negative ($\beta = - 0.51$, $p < 0.05$).

According to hypothesis 1, IWE is strongly and negatively associated with workplace deviance. To test this hypothesis, Model 4 as well as and Model 5 in Table 3.3.5 were employed. The results, for Model 4 Table 3.3.5, show a significant but negative relationship between IWE and workplace deviance ($\beta = -0.23$, $p < 0.05$). Similarly, for Model 5 Table 3.3.5, the relationship between IWE and deviance is significant and negative ($\beta = -0.27$, $p < 0.05$). These results demonstrate that IWE is significantly and negatively related to workplace deviance. Thus, hypothesis 1 is empirically supported. It means that workers with high IWE do not show workplace deviance and it is consistent with previous empirical findings (Javed et al., 2019). For the same Model 5 Table 3.3.5, the result shows a positive and very significant relationship between employee hostility and workplace deviance ($\beta = 0.34$, $p < 0.001$). Therefore, it demonstrates that hostility has a very strong relationship with workplace deviance.

Table 3.3.5

Regression Results

Variable	Hostility		Workplace deviance		
	Model 1	Model 2	Model 3	Model 4	Model 5
Generalized Self Efficacy (GSE)	0.15*	0.11	-0.28**	-0.19*	-0.22*
Employee Age	-0.04	-0.04	-0.10	-0.08	-0.07
Employee Gender	0.16	0.14	-0.51*	-0.45**	-0.50**
Experience Under Current Supervisor	0.01	0.01	-0.08	-0.08	-0.08
Employee Experience	-0.07	-0.06	0.19	0.17	0.19
Islamic Work Ethics (IWE)	-	0.10	-	-0.23*	-0.27*
Hostility	-	-	-	-	0.34***
R^2	0.05	0.05	0.13	0.15	0.22

Notes: N = 189, * p < 0.05, ** p < 0.01, ***p < 0.001.

According to the hypothesis 2, employee perceived abusive supervision moderates the indirect effect of Islamic work ethics on workplace deviance through hostility. This hypothesis was tested by employing the moderated mediation model of the SPSS PROCESS proposed by Hayes and Preacher (2014). The variables were mean-centered. The Model 6 and Model 7, in Table 3.3.6 show mediation and moderation results respectively.

Table 3.3.6

Regression Results

Variable	Hostility	Workplace Deviance
	Model 6	Model 7
Generalized Self Efficacy (GSE)	0.14*	-0.22
Employee Age	-0.05	-0.07
Employee Gender	0.35**	-0.50
Experience Under Current Supervisor	0.03	-0.08
Employee Experience	0.06	0.19
Islamic Work Ethics (IWE)	0.23*	-0.27*
Perceived Abusive Supervision (AS)	0.38***	-
IWE x AS	0.39***	-
Hostility	-	0.34***
R^2	0.38	0.22

Notes: N=189; * p < 0.05, ** p < .01), *** p < .001.

3.3.4.1 Mediating Role of Employee Hostility

Table 3.3.6 shows the test results of the mediating role played by employee hostility between IWE and workplace deviance in the presence of employee perceived abusive supervision. The Model 6 Table 3.3.6 shows a very significant and positive joint effect of IWE and abusive supervision on hostility ($\beta = 0.39$, $p < 0.001$). These results also indicate that the relationship between IWE and workplace deviance through hostility is significant and negative ($\beta = -0.27$, $p < 0.05$). The Model 7 Table 3.3.6 shows that employee's hostility is very significantly and positively related to workplace deviance ($\beta = 0.34$, $p < 0.001$).

Thus, these findings confirm the mediating role of employee hostility between IWE and workplace deviance in the presence of employee perceived abusive supervision.

3.3.4.2 Moderating Role of Employee Perceived Abusive Supervision

Lastly, to confirm the results, the conditional indirect effect of IWE on workplace deviance through employees' hostility was investigated at three levels. Table 3.3.7 demonstrates the results of the indirect effects measured to study conditional indirect effect of IWE on workplace deviance through hostility at the low, mean and high level of employee perceived abusive supervision. The conditional indirect effect of IWE on workplace deviance is insignificant (including zero) for low values (-1 SD) of employee perceived abusive supervision ($\beta = -0.02$, 95% CI [-0.11, 0.05]). However, it becomes significant (not including zero) for higher values (+1 SD) of employee perceived abusive supervision ($\beta = 0.18$, 95% CI [0.08, 0.30]).

Thus, these results demonstrate that the indirect effect of IWE on workplace deviance through hostility changes its direction from negative to positive, and it is significant when abusive supervision is at the higher, but not at the lower level. This indicates that employees' perceived abusive supervision plays a moderating role between IWE and workplace deviance through hostility.

These results verify that employee's perceived abusive supervision moderates the indirect effect of IWE on workplace deviance through hostility. This indirect effect of IWE on workplace deviance thorough hostility is significant when their perceived abusive supervision is high rather than low. Consequently, the index of moderated mediation confirms that hypothesis 2 is empirically supported.

Table 3.3.7

Indirect Effect of IWE on Workplace Deviance through Hostility at Various Levels of Perceived Abusive Supervision

Perceived Abusive Supervision	In-direct Effect	SE	95% Bias-Corrected CI	
			Lower	Upper
Low	-0.02	0.04	-0.11	0.05
Mean	0.08	0.03	0.02	0.16
High	0.18	0.06	0.08	0.30

The impact of IWE on employee hostility at a high and low level of employee perceived abusive supervision is illustrated in Figure 4. This figure indicates that the effect of IWE on hostility increases when the level of employee perceived abusive supervision is higher. This effect does not hold for the low level of their perceived abusive supervision. It means that the IWE is either negatively related or not related to workplace deviance at all, when perceived abusive supervision is low. On the other hand, when employees are subjected to high abusive supervisory behavior, they become hostile and show workplace deviance.

Figure 4

Two-Way Interaction Effects

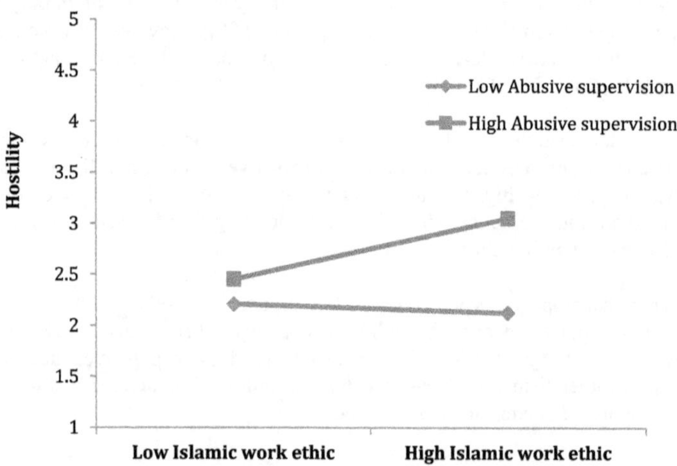

The results of the study are graphically illustrated in Figure 4. The lower curve shows the impact of low abusive supervision on the link between IWE and deviance by way of hostility. The curve shows a downward trend. This means that when employee' perceived abusive supervision is low, through hostility, they are less inclined toward workplace deviance. These results are in conformity with the results of similar studies (e.g., Golparvar & Nadi, 2011; Bhatti et al., 2016).

The higher curve shows the impact of high abusive supervision on the link between IWE and deviance passing through hostility. The curve visibly shows an upward trend. It means that when employee' perceived abusive supervision is high, through hostility, they are more inclined toward workplace deviance.

Thus, Figure 4 clearly illustrates a change in direction of the relationship between Islamic work ethics and workplace deviance through hostility, when employees' perceived abusive supervision is higher. These new findings would contribute toward expanding the Islamic work ethics and workplace deviance related literature.

The conditional effect of IWE on employees' hostility at the values of abusive supervision is calculated through SPSS PROCESS using the Johnson-Neyman technique.

Table 3.3.8

Conditional Effect of IWE on Employees' Hostility at Values of Abusive Supervision

Abusive Supervision	Effect on Hostility	Standard Error	t-statistic	p-value	LLCI	ULCI
-1.65	-0.42	0.18	-2.34	0.02	-0.78	-0.07
-1.46	-0.35	0.16	-2.11	0.04	-0.67	-0.02
-1.36	-0.31	0.16	-1.97	0.05	-0.62	0.00
-1.28	-0.27	0.15	-1.84	0.07	-0.57	0.02
-1.09	-0.20	0.13	-1.49	0.14	-0.47	0.07
-0.90	-0.13	0.12	-1.05	0.29	-0.37	0.11
-0.72	-0.05	0.11	-0.50	0.62	-0.27	0.16
-0.53	0.02	0.10	0.19	0.85	-0.17	0.21
-0.34	0.09	0.09	1.04	0.30	-0.08	0.27
-0.17	0.16	0.08	1.97	0.05	0.00	0.32
-0.16	0.17	0.08	2.03	0.04	0.00	0.33
0.03	0.24	0.08	3.05	0.00	0.08	0.39
0.22	0.31	0.08	3.97	0.00	0.16	0.47
0.40	0.38	0.08	4.65	0.00	0.22	0.55
0.59	0.46	0.09	5.09	0.00	0.28	0.64
0.78	0.53	0.10	5.33	0.00	0.33	0.73
0.96	0.60	0.11	5.43	0.00	0.38	0.82
1.15	0.68	0.12	5.45	0.00	0.43	0.92
1.34	0.75	0.14	5.44	0.00	0.48	1.02
1.52	0.82	0.15	5.40	0.00	0.52	1.13
1.71	0.90	0.17	5.35	0.00	0.57	1.23
1.90	0.97	0.18	5.30	0.00	0.61	1.33
2.08	1.04	0.20	5.25	0.00	0.65	1.44

The results shown in Table 3.3.8 indicate that hostility of employees possessing IWE increases with an increase in abusive supervision. LLCI stands for the lower level of confidence interval and ULCI stands for the upper level of confidence interval.

3.3.5 Discussion

Recently, some scholars have investigated the impact of IWE on job-related behaviors and outcomes (Yousef, 2000b & 2001; Ahmad, 2011). In spite of these studies, the likely effects of IWE on workplace deviance in the presence of employee perceived abusive supervision and employee hostility were not found in the literature. In an effort to bridge this research gap, the study explored whether IWE causes a change in workplace deviance in the presence of employees' perceived abusive supervision and hostility.

The study aligns with the research that investigates the combined effect of employee personality and perceptions of work situations with their workplace deviance (e.g., Colbert et al., 2004) as well as with the literature that takes into account the ethical belief of employees as an antecedent of their workplace deviance (e.g., Henle et al., 2005; Treviño et al., 2006).

The results show that IWE is significantly and negatively related to workplace deviance. So, IWE is linked with a decrease in workplace deviance. As Islam directs its followers to work with full devotion and dedication, it might be anticipated that employees with a higher level of IWE would tend to stick more to the prescribed course of action provided by their supervisors, as compared to the individuals with a low degree of IWE. These results show one side of Islamic philosophy and teachings and are in-line with the previous literature showing positive job outcomes.

Findings of the study also suggest that employee perceived abusive supervision moderates the indirect effect of IWE on workplace deviance through hostility. These findings may be explained with the view that teachings of Islam encourage followers to be loyal to their employer and respect and appreciate their leader in the workplace, and both leaders and followers should be considered as brothers (Mohammad & Quoquab, 2016). Followers of this philosophy intend to bring good for them, for their organization and society (Ahmad, 2011; Murtaza et al., 2016).

Finally, the findings suggest that the indirect effect of IWE on workplace deviance thorough hostility is significant when employees' perceived abusive supervision is high rather than low. These results may be justified with the help of a key Islamic principle of "enjoining what is right and forbidding what is wrong" which has repeatedly been mentioned in the Holy Qur'an and in the tradition of the Holy Prophet Muhammad (May Allah have peace be upon Him and His Family). It shows a different perspective of Islamic philosophy and thought, which to one's surprise, is missing in the literature. This study takes the lead and brings forth this relationship empirically for the first time.

The findings are also consistent with social exchange theory (Homans, 1958) and norm of reciprocity theory presented by Gouldner (1960). The aim of the study was to explore the relationship between IWE and workplace deviance through employee perceived abusive supervision and hostility. The social exchange theory (Homans, 1958) argued that social transactions between two parties occurred and each one tried to increase benefits and decrease costs associated with that transaction. As expected, IWE was found significantly and negatively related to employee workplace deviance. It was found that employees possessing high IWE adhered strongly to the course of action provided by their employer with an intention to efficiently bring good for the workplace and its members. So, they were less inclined to workplace deviance. Employees may consider leader mistreatment or abusive behavior as injustice in the workplace that may cause feelings of stress and hostility. It would not be a surprise if victimized or observing employees with high IWE and hostility show workplace deviance. They might be sensitive towards abusive supervision which would cause hostility and eventually deviance (Mayer et al., 2012). Therefore, the followers with high IWE, still intending to bring good to the workplace, might directly and forcefully confront the transgressors by demonstrating workplace deviance. This increased level of workplace deviance is significant when employees perceived abusive supervision is high.

3.4 Study 3: Impact of Islamic Work Ethics (IWE) on Employee Prohibitive Voice Behavior (PVB)

3.4.1 Sample and Procedures

The population of the study is all full-time managers or supervisors and employees working in the private sector organizations, operating in or around the city of Lahore, Pakistan. The rationale behind collecting data from diverse sectors is to increase the generalizability of the study and not to limit the study to only one sector or industry.

Self-administered questionnaires, written in English and coded for proper matching, were handed over to 250 private-sector employees. The respondents were full-time employees of organizations specializing in manufacturing, engineering, transportation, banking, and information technology in the private sector of Pakistan. The data collection was performed in and around Lahore, which is the capital of the largest province, the Punjab, and the second-largest city of the country.

A cover letter that stated the purpose of the study and guaranteed respondents' secrecy and anonymity was distributed with the questionnaires. Out of the total 250, 189 completed surveys were received. Only those surveys were included in the analysis where responses received were from one supervisor and at least two or more matching subordinates working under the same supervisor. This response rate (76%) is in line with other studies performed in a similar context (Raja et al., 2004; Abbas et al., 2014). Results revealed by demographics confirmed that a large percentage (87%) of the respondents were males.

Common method bias, as proposed by Podsakoff and colleagues (2003), was avoided by collecting data in two waves which were at least one month apart.

At wave one; responses were recorded from supervisors and subordinates. The supervisors were requested to respond to performance-related items for an arbitrary sample of their assigned employees. Later on, the same set of employees working under the same supervisor were requested to complete surveys containing items relating to IWE, their demographics (e.g., age, gender, experience under the current supervisor, total professional experience, and their hierarchical level). After one month, at wave two, the same set of subordinates was requested to respond to items related to voice behavior.

3.4.2 Measures

All items used in the questionnaires were placed on a five point Likert-type scale, that ranged from 1=strongly disagree to 5=strongly agree. The scales and items that were used to measure variables are discussed below.

3.4.2.1 Islamic Work Ethics (IWE)

The scale, proposed by Ali (1988), consisting of 17 items was employed to measure IWE. Item 9 was reverse coded. Cranach's alpha for the scale was 0.90. The following items were used:

1. Laziness is a vice (defect).

2. Dedication to work is a virtue (good behavior).

3. Good work benefits both one's self and others.

4. Justice and generosity in the work place are necessary conditions for society's welfare.

5. Producing more than enough to meet one's personal needs contributes to the prosperity of society as a whole.

6. One should carry work out to the best of one's ability.

7. Work is not an end in itself but a means to foster personal growth and social relations.

8. Life has no meaning without work.

9. More leisure time is good for society. (Reverse coded)

10. Human relations in organizations should be emphasized and encouraged.

11. Work enables man to control nature.

12. Creative work is a source of happiness and accomplishment.

13. Any man who works is more likely to get ahead in life.

14. Work gives one the chance to be independent.

15. A successful man is the one who meets deadlines at work.

16. One should constantly work hard to meet responsibilities.

17. The value of work is derived from the accompanying intentions rather than the results.

3.4.2.2 Prohibitive Voice Behavior (PVB)

Employee prohibitive voice behavior was gauged using the 5-item scale introduced by Liang and colleagues (2012). Cronbach's alpha for the scale was 0.72. The following items were used:

1. I advise other colleagues against undesirable behaviors that would hamper job performance.

2. I speak up honestly with problems that might cause serious loss to the organization, even when dissenting (disagreeing) opinions exist.

3. I dare to voice out opinions on things that might affect efficiency in the organization, even if that would embarrass others.

4. I dare to point out problems when they appear in the organization, even if that would hamper relationships with other colleagues.

5. I proactively report coordination problems in the workplace to the management.

3.4.2.3 Employee Generalized Self-Efficacy (GSE)

To take changes in the competency level of employees that might affect their predicted behavior into account employees' GSE was also controlled for (Judge et al., 2000). GSE was measured using a scale adapted from the eight-item measure developed by Judge and colleagues (2000). Item number two, four, five and seven were reverse coded. Cronbach's alpha for the scale was 0.70. The following items of the GSE scale were included.

1. I am strong enough to overcome life's struggles.

2. At root (basically), I am a weak person. (Reverse coded)

3. I can handle the situations that life brings.

4. I usually feel that I am an unsuccessful person. (Reverse coded)

5. I often feel that there is nothing that I can do well. (Reverse coded)

6. I feel competent to deal effectively with the real world.

7. I often feel like a failure. (Reverse coded)

8. I usually feel I can handle the typical problems that come up in life.

3.4.2.4 Control Variables

The following variables were controlled for as these could affect the findings of this study: generalized self-efficacy of employees, age of subordinates, the gender of subordinates, qualification of subordinates, the experience of subordinates under the current supervisor, and subordinate's hierarchical level in the organization (LePine & Van Dyne, 1998).

3.4.3 Results

Results of the study were measured in two main stages. Initially, the confirmatory factor analysis (CFA) was conducted to evaluate factor configuration along with the discriminant validity of the main scales—IWE and PVB. AMOS with maximum likelihood estimation was employed to assess the model fitness (Arbuckle & Wothke, 1999). To test the proposed hypothesis, simple regression was run at the second stage of the analysis.

3.4.3.1 Confirmatory Factor Analysis (CFA)

Confirmatory factor analysis (CFA) was performed to verify convergent and discriminant validity of the study variables by ensuring that the data followed the assumption that all of the employed variables represented distinct constructs. Convergent validity of the variables was verified through the factor loading score of each item on its respective construct (Parasuraman et al., 2002; Park et al., 2006).

While dealing with a scale comprising a large number of items to explain a specific construct, the issue of inflated measurement errors may arise (Judge et al., 2002). This issue would cause an unfavorable effect on the fitness of the model which could be addressed by applying the parceling technique (Smith & Webster, 2017). Employing this technique, the constructs of the IWE scale were grouped into parcels. The heterogeneous assignment of items (Cole et al., 2016) was used, which allowed varying numbers of items in different parcels. The 17-item IWE scale was packed into a total of four parcels. On the basis of low factor loadings, four items were excluded from the analysis.

To evaluate the model fitness in CFA, the Chi-Square Statistic, Root Mean Square Error of Approximation (RMSEA; acceptable fit: 0.05 – 0.08), the Standardized Root Mean Square Residual (SRMR; acceptable fit: 0.05 – 0.10, good fit: 0 – 0.08), the Comparative Fit Index (CFI; acceptable fit: 0.90– 0.97, good fit: 0.97–1) and the Tucker-Lewis Index (TLI; acceptable fit: greater than 0.90; Bentler & Bonett, 1980; Bentler, 1990; Hu & Bentler, 1999; Schermelleh-Engel et al., 2003; Marsh et al., 2004; Chen et al., 2008) were used.

Table 3.4.1

CFA Measurement Models

Model	Factors	CMIN/df	RMSEA	CFI	RMR	TLI
1	Proposed three factors	73.45 / 34 = 2.16	0.08	0.94	0.04	0.92
2	One factor	205.47 / 36 = 5.71	0.16	0.73	0.11	0.66

As shown in Table 3.3.1, these indices evidenced a good fit of the proposed model. The proposed model of all factors, vis-à-vis the one-factor model, indicated a considerably better fit. The discriminant validity of all three scales was, thus, confirmed by the CFA results. For Model 1, all of the fit statistics were satisfactory (CMIN/df = 2.16, p < 0.10, CFI = 0.94, RMSEA = 0.08, RMR = 0.04, TLI = 0.92). The CFA results confirmed the convergent as well as the discriminant validity of the study variables. Therefore, the CFA results indicated that the collected data were suitable for hypotheses testing.

3.4.3.2 Demographic Information, Descriptive Statistics, Reliability and Correlation Results

The demographic information is presented in Table 3.4.2. The descriptive statistics of all demographic variables are given in Table 3.4.3.

Table 3.4.2

Demographic Information

Variable		Frequency	Percentage
Age	Less than 25 years	54	28.6
	25-30 years	86	45.5
	31-34 years	31	16.4
	35-40 years	12	6.3
	41-44 years	2	1.1
	45-50 years	1	0.5
	51-54 years	1	0.5
	55 years and above	2	1.1
Gender	Male	164	86.8
	Female	25	13.2
	Qualification		
	Intermediate	28	14.8
	Bachelors	87	46.0
	Masters	74	39.2
Experience Under Current Supervisor	Less than a year	77	40.7
	1-2 years	62	32.8
	3-5 years	37	19.6
	6-10 years	11	5.8
	More than 10 years	2	1.1
Hierarchy	Entry level	70	37.0
	Middle level	100	52.9
	Senior level	19	10.1
Note: N = 189			

The descriptive statistics of the controlled for and observed variables are given in the following Table 3.4.3. The correlations between the control variables (employee age, gender, qualification, experience under current supervisor, hierarchy) with the main study variables are also given in Table 3.4.4. Employee age, job experience and experience of the employee under the current supervisor are stated in years.

Table 3.4.3

Descriptive Statistics

Variable	Mean	Standard Deviation	Minimum	Maximum
Age	26	5.18	1	8
Gender	1.13	0.34	1	2
Qualification	2.24	0.69	1	3
Experience Under Current Supervisor	1.94	0.97	1	5
Hierarchy	1.73	0.63	1	3
Generalized Self Efficacy (GSE)	3.60	0.69	1.5	5
Islamic Work Ethics	3.73	0.57	2	5
Prohibitive Voice Behavior	3.33	0.66	1	5
Note: N = 189				

The correlations of the control and the main variables of the proposed model are shown in Table 3.4.4. According to the correlation tests, as predicted, IWE was positively correlated with the employees' PVB ($r = 0.34$, $p < 0.01$). These correlation results were according to the proposed model and encouraged us to move forward and test the hypotheses.

Table 3.4.4

Correlations Analysis

Variable	1	2	3	4	5	6	7
Islamic Work Ethic	-						
Prohibitive Voice Behavior	0.34**	-					
Generalized Self Efficacy	0.49**	0.235**	-				
Age (a)	0.09	0.11	0.14				
Gender (b)	0.15*	0.12	0.02	-0.12			
Qualification (c)	-0.04	0.02	-0.01	-0.01	0.13		
Experience Under Current Supervisor (d)	-0.03	0.07	-0.01	0.31**	0.03	0.29**	
Hierarchy (e)	0.06	-0.03	0.15*	0.32**	-0.01	0.17*	.38**

Notes: * $p < 0.05$, ** $p < 0.01$

(a) Age codes: 1 = Less than 25 years, 2 = 25-30 years, 3 = 31-34 years, 4 = 35-40 years, 5 = 41-44 years, 6 = 45-50 years, 7 = 51-54 years, 8 = 55 years and above.

(b) Gender codes: 1 = Male, 2 = Female.

(c) Qualification codes: 1 = Intermediate, 2 = Bachelor's, 3 = Masters, 4 = Doctorate.

(d) Experience under current supervisor codes: 1 = less than a year, 2 = 1–2 years, 3 = 3–5 years, 4 = 6–10 years, 5 = more than 10 years

(e) Hierarchical level codes: 1 = Entry level, 2 = Middle level, 3 = Senior level

Cronbach's alpha reliability of the main study variables: generalized self-efficacy, Islamic work ethics and prohibitive voice behavior, is stated in the Table 3.4.5.

Table 3.4.5

Cronbach's Alpha Reliability

Sr. No.	Constructs	No. of Items	Cronbach's Alpha Value
1.	**Generalized Self Efficacy**	8	0.70
2.	**Islamic Work Ethics**	17	0.90
3.	**Prohibitive Voice Behavior**	5	0.72

Note: N = 189

3.4.4 Hypothesis Testing

Hypothesis 1 presented in this study takes into account the effect of IWE on predicting employees' voice behavior.

A two-level model was employed to test the proposed hypothesis. Only elements controlled for variables, including generalized self-efficacy, were entered to calculate results for Model 1. However, all the controlled for variables, including generalized self-efficacy, along with IWE were entered to calculate results for Model 2.

To calculate results, linear regressions were run. Table 3.4.6 enlists test results of the impact of the controlled for variables and IWE on the PVB.

Table 3.4.6

Regression Results

Variable	Prohibitive Voice Behavior (PVB)	
	Model 1	**Model 2**
Age	0.08	0.07
Gender	0.27	0.15
Qualification	0.03	0.04
Hierarchical level	-0.12	-0.11
Generalized Self Efficacy	0.22***	0.09
Islamic work ethic	-	0.32***
R^2	.09	.15

Notes: $N = 189$; * $p < 0.05$, ** $p < 0.01$, *** $p < 0.001$.

Model 1 in Table 3.4.6 shows the effects of all control variables on subordinate prohibitive voice behavior which is significantly and positively related to GSE of employees ($\beta = 0.22$, $p < 0.001$). This indicates that employees with GSE demonstrate PVB in the workplace.

Model 2 shows the effect of control variables and IWE on prohibitive voice behavior (PVB) of employees. The regression results demonstrate that PVB of employees is positively and significantly related with the employees IWE ($\beta = 0.32$, $p < 0.01$). These findings confirm that employees who possess IWE are more likely to demonstrate strong prohibitive voice behavior in the workplace. These results of Model 1 and Model 2, listed in Table 3.4.6, empirically support the proposed hypothesis 1.

3.4.5 Discussion

Employee voice has been viewed as an optional behavior expressed by them that depended upon their complex "cognitive processes" (Chiaburu et al., 2008). The present study attempted to link IWE, which is a cognitive process, with the PVB of employees. It contributed by verifying the conceptual model that helped to explain how IWE was linked with PVB of employees. It also helped to identify IWE as an antecedent of the employee PVB. The study suggested and confirmed that subordinates who possessed IWE proactively spoke up in the workplace.

The test result of the study verified IWE as a predictor of employee voice behavior. So, this study is in line with other similar studies (e.g., LePine & Van Dyne, 1998; Chiaburu et al., 2008; Liang et al., 2012) that explored predictors of employee voice behavior. By presenting a new and somewhat less discussed antecedent of the PVB, this study added value to the existing workplace voice behavior-related literature.

Furthermore, the results showed some key theory implications. Since IWE has its roots in the belief system of the workforce, it might lead its followers to ethically behave and positively contribute in the workplace. In addition, it could proactively protect the workforce and the workplace from potentially harmful circumstances and behaviors. Thus, IWE has the ability to provide a shield against some potentially harmful effects that might be caused by employees' action or behavior in the workplace.

The research was conducted in a relatively less explored context of Pakistan. Therefore, by enhancing its generalizability, the study would add value to existing employee voice-related literature.

3.5 Chapter Summary

The data, related to each study, were analyzed using regression analysis to test the theoretical models and proposed hypotheses of all three studies. The hypotheses were proposed to test the following relationships: Islamic work ethics are significantly and negatively related to workplace deviance. Workplace deviance is significantly and positively related to employees' perceived abusive supervision. The relationship between Islamic work ethics and employees' perceived abusive supervision is mediated by workplace deviance. Employee perceived abusive supervision moderates the indirect effect of IWE on workplace deviance through hostility. The indirect effect of IWE on workplace deviance thorough hostility is significant when employees' perceived abusive supervision is high rather than low. Islamic work ethics are significantly and positively related to prohibitive voice behavior of employees. The results indicate that all of these relationships proposed in each study are empirically verified.

The next chapter, Chapter 4, discusses the conclusion and managerial implications of the results of each study presented in this chapter, Chapter 3.

Chapter 4

Conclusion

4.1 Introduction

The previous chapter presented the results of the correlations and hypothesized relationships of all three studies. The previous chapter presented the statistical results of each study and discussion related to these obtained results in the light of theory and the context of the study. Thus, this chapter will discuss the conclusion of all studies. In addition, the contribution of these studies, some managerial implications, and future research possibilities are discussed. As the aim of the research was to examine the role of employee personality, workplace mistreatment, and job outcomes, the discussion focuses on the same. Moreover, the chapter discusses the findings with a backdrop of contextual factors that can potentially influence the relationships among employee personality, workplace mistreatment, and job outcomes.

The following section of the chapter discusses the conclusions, managerial implications and future research directions related to the first study.

4.2 Study 1: Islamic Work Ethics and Workplace Deviance: Antecedents of Abusive Supervision

4.2.1 Conclusion

Perceived abusive supervision adversely affects organizational well-being as it is believed to be associated with many negative job-related outcomes (e.g., low productivity and creativity, WD, low innovation). The findings highlight that IWE is linked with lower WD and this deviance is positively linked with perceived abusive supervision. Additionally, when subordinates demonstrate a higher degree of deviant behavior, they attract more supervisory abuse. IWE plays its role in decreasing WD, which in turn decreases the level of supervisory abuse. These results are useful as they attract the focus of researchers and practitioners toward relatively less-explored predictors of the perceptions and effects of supervisory abuse in the workplace. Making use of the findings of the study, the business managers would be able to devise realistic interventions to reduce the severity and incidence of perceived supervisory abuse in the workplace. Management of organization could properly train supervisors to improve or eliminate perceptions of subordinates about supervisors' behavior. This could lead to a more productive and efficient workplace.

4.2.2 Managerial Implications

It might be argued that IWE could provide a shield against potentially damaging behaviors of individuals or groups of individuals in the workplace. Business managers could utilize these results to protect the workplace.

Abusive supervision may badly affect an organization's profitability (Tepper, 2007; Henle & Gross, 2014). Using these findings, business managers could predict and proactively act to curb abusive behavior. Managers may create a more favorable environment by placing employees who demonstrate good work ethics in key positions. They could place appropriate checks while recruiting, selecting, transferring or promoting employees in the organization. Consequently, these suitably-placed employees would tend to stick to the given course of action, SOP, and be less deviant.

Abusive supervision, if left unchecked, could prove to be counter-productive and damaging for the organizations. Victimized employees could file costly lawsuits against supervisors or organizations. Thus, the managers should preemptively avoid the occurrence of WD. It is suggested that employees with higher IWE should be welcomed and encouraged in the workplace to reduce WD. A reduced level of WD would in turn reduce or eliminate abusive supervision.

4.2.3 Future Research Directions

Some limitations of this study that could offer new opportunities for future research are discussed in this section. An increased number of responses would likely improve results. The value of related research would increase if more religious, cultural, national, institutional, and economic contexts are taken into account.

Podsakoff and colleagues (2003) suggest the possibility of common method bias associated with self-reported data. However, Conway and Lance (2010) suggest that, in some cases, self-reported data would be considered "appropriate" and "theoretically relevant". It is suggested that IWE and perceived abusive supervision are directly associated with employees themselves. Therefore, it would be appropriate and relevant to use the self-reported data in this case.

It may be argued that perceived employees' abusive supervision could be different than the actual. The adopted approach is in accordance with a general agreement among researchers that supervisory abuse is based on employee perceptions (Mitchell &

Ambrose, 2007). Indeed, some over-sensitive individuals may perceive abuse even in situations where there is no abuse (Aquino & Lamertz, 2004). To further improve results, future research could explore abusive supervision more independently by collecting data from alternative sources.

Future studies might also investigate other important outcome variables (e.g., corporate citizenship behavior, voice, silence, turnover intentions) which might act as antecedents of perceived abusive supervision. While contributing to achieving a better workplace, the study could open new research avenues.

The following section of the chapter discusses the conclusions, managerial implications and future research directions related to the second study.

4.3 Study 2: Islamic Work Ethics and Workplace Deviance: Moderated by Abusive Supervision and Mediated by Employee Hostility

4.3.1 Conclusion

The relationship between IWE and workplace deviance, in the presence of employee perceived, abusive supervision and hostility maybe explained through the norm of reciprocity, the theory presented by Gouldner (1960). Employing the norm of reciprocity theory, it may be proposed that when subordinates with high IWE are subjected to abusive supervisory behavior, they will retaliate in return, due to their unique personality characteristics, still with an intention to bring good for the workplace and its members. Also, in these conditions, they would be inclined to deviate from the guidelines provided to them by their abusing supervisors. The findings confirmed that employee perceived abusive supervision moderates the indirect effect of Islamic work ethics on workplace deviance through hostility. Furthermore, the indirect effect of IWE on workplace deviance through hostility is significant when employees' perceived abusive supervision is high rather than low.

On the whole, the study reveals some significant findings. It shows the ability of IWE to recognize and predict an important employee behavior, i.e. workplace deviance. Also, it shows that the relationship between IWE and workplace deviance is moderated by employee perceived abusive supervision. Additionally, this study verifies that the said relation is mediated by employee hostility. Furthermore, the study challenges a widely held assumption that has led many, if not all, researchers to believe that the IWE-related job outcomes will follow a certain predictable direction. The researchers seemed to assume that IWE would always contribute either positively towards those job outcomes that were to bring good or contribute negatively towards those job outcomes which were to bring harm to the organization. This study confirms that there could be some situations in which the previously held assumption was not valid. However, these findings are still explainable with the help of the teachings of Islam.

This research is expected to contribute to the body of scholarly knowledge in numerous ways. By identifying IWE as an antecedent of workplace deviance, it will become a part of the literature that deals with antecedents of workplace deviance. The study confirms reversal of the conventional relationship between IWE and workplace deviance when employee's perceived abusive supervision is high. The results of the study verify the moderating role of employee perceived abusive supervision on the relationship between IWE and workplace deviance. Furthermore, it is confirmed that the relationship between IWE and workplace deviance is mediated by employee hostility.

As mentioned above, the study challenges a general assumption held by many researchers that IWE-related job outcomes always follow a certain predictable direction to demonstrate a positive contribution to the organization. On the contrary, the results of the study confirm that at a higher degree of perceived abusive supervision, employee hostility starts playing its role. At this stage, the relationship between IWE and WD becomes significant while reversing its initial direction. Even though these results are in conflict with the previous research, they are still explainable within the domain of Islamic philosophy. Therefore, this study could potentially break the existing psychological barriers in the way of the IWE-related research.

4.3.2 Managerial Implications

The study could be very helpful for business managers, human resource professionals, headhunters, or practitioners at the time of, including but not limited to, recruiting, selecting, training, posting, transferring, or promoting workforce. Organizations would like to curb negative job outcomes to increase efficiency and productivity while cutting down their costs associated with recruitment, selection, and training of employees. The study could help managers to predict the behavior of the potential workforce if it is likely to face abusive supervision in the workplace.

The organizations operating or planning to operate in a Muslim country (e.g., Pakistan) are likely to hire Muslim workers. Therefore, this study could help business managers of these organizations to better understand on job behavior of their current or potential workforce.

Managers may avoid or reduce perceptions of abusive supervision and workplace deviance by placing individuals with high IWE in their organization. This action could create a self-correcting and an auto-improving mechanism in the workplace. It could also contribute toward achieving an increased level of efficiency and productivity and a better workplace due to fewer deviant employees and a low degree of perceived abusive supervision.

4.3.3 Future Research Directions

Similar to any other research, this study is not immune to limitations. Some of these are the following. First, to improve the generalizability of the study, the number of responses could be increased to take into account a larger sample of employees working in other industries.

Second, the reliability and general acceptability of the research findings may be increased by collecting data from other countries where the population of the workforce is predominantly Muslim. However, there still might be some workplace factors that are only valid in the context of Pakistan.

Third, future studies might include other variables (e.g., corporate citizenship behavior, turnover intentions, and job commitment) which may be moderated by perceived abusive supervision.

Finally, as suggested by (Podsakoff et al., 2003), there could be a common-method bias associated with self-reported data. IWE, perceived abusive supervision, and hostility are associated with subordinates themselves. Deviant workplace behavior is less likely to be shown openly in public. But, Conway and Lance (2010) suggest that in some cases, self-reported data could be considered "appropriate" and "theoretically relevant". Thus, it would seem fit to use this method of measurement. Moreover, complex models, such as the proposed moderated mediation model, are less likely to have common method bias (Podsakoff et al., 2003).

Even though several research articles have explored the effect of IWE on many job-related outcomes, it would be useful to pay more attention to the role played by IWE and perceived abusive supervision on other personality traits or personality states of the workforce. Forthcoming research may explore the role performed by IWE and the effects of workplace mistreatment upon some other significant workplace-related behaviors and issues. Furthermore, since IWE has its base in the beliefs of the workforce, it might have potential not only to lead its followers towards behaving and contributing positively to the workplace, but also to encourage them to protect the workforce and the workplace from potentially harmful circumstances or behaviors of other individuals or group of individuals at both the horizontal or vertical levels. IWE might also provide a shield against potentially damaging effects of various behaviors of other individuals or groups of individuals in the workplace. This study can open new avenues for future research, contributing to achieving a better workplace for tomorrow.

The following section discusses the conclusions, managerial implications and future research directions related to the third study.

4.4 Study 3: Islamic Work Ethics and Employee Prohibitive Voice Behavior

4.4.1 Conclusion

This study highlights and verifies a role played by IWE in predicting voice behavior. The findings of this study empirically confirm that IWE is significantly and positively related to employees' prohibitive voice behavior (PVB). Employees who possess a higher degree of IWE strongly raise their voice in the workplace. Therefore, Islamic work ethics can be considered as an antecedent of a relatively less-explored voice behavior of employees. This workplace behavior ignites a cognitive process in employees who intend to proactively protect their workplace from potentially harmful outcomes. Consequently, the employees who possess a higher degree of IWE are more inclined to proactively display prohibitive voice behavior in the workplace.

Business managers can develop practical and a proactive approach to introduce or promote a whistleblowing culture in their organizations which autocorrects their workplace. They can achieve favorable outcomes by placing employees with higher IWE in the organization. This will increase the likelihood of whistleblowing or PVB in the workplace. The decision-makers can formulate effective plans and policies to promote employees' PVB in the organization by training or hiring employees who possess management's preferred workplace ethics.

4.4.2 Managerial Implications

Workplace voice behavior is an important job outcome and has been investigated by many scholars (e.g., LePine & Van Dyne, 1998; Chiaburu et al., 2008; Liang et al., 2012; Peng & Wei, 2019). It would be valuable for practitioners to predict and proactively prepare themselves for an expected voice behavior of employees. Findings of this study can provide useful suggestions for the managers to help them anticipate the PVB of employees. Making use of these findings, managers may adopt appropriate measures in advance to benefit from or effectively respond to this behavior. Business managers may focus on creating an environment in the workplace by thoughtfully placing employees who possess Islamic work ethics. These employees would demonstrate a higher tendency to proactively speak-up. This can help managers to create a kind of alarm system in the organization that sets off when some potentially harmful actions or behaviors are detected in the workplace.

Managers may put appropriate checks in place while recruiting, selecting, transferring or promoting employees in the organization. Proper training of employees could be another approach that managers could adopt to help employees transform their work ethics for the larger interest of the organization. This would help subordinates to constructively modify their thoughts so they could raise a proactive voice as whistleblowers with an intention to bring good for their organization and its members.

As it is argued in this study that employees with higher IWE would show stronger proactive and prohibitive voice behavior, so in the presence of some unpleasant situation, they are likely to talk louder with an intention to correct and improve the present state of affairs in their workplace. Thus, in order to support the PVB of employees, managers may hire or train a workforce that possesses strong Islamic work ethics. As a result, it could give their organization a competitive edge by nurturing the workforce that demonstrates a self-correcting mechanism.

4.4.3 Future Research Directions

Following are some directions and limitations of the study which could offer new opportunities for future research. First, to further improve the generalizability of the study, the number of responses may be increased. In addition, if more religious, cultural, national, institutional, and economic diversity is taken into account, the results would show a wider acceptability.

As mentioned above, according to Podsakoff et al. (2003), there could be a common-method bias associated with self-reported data. Conway and Lance (2010), on the other hand, suggest that in some cases self-reported data could be considered "appropriate" and "theoretically relevant". The IWE and PVB were explored by adopting measures that required self-reporting by subordinates, it would be appropriate and relevant to use this method of measurement.

Future studies might investigate a few other important workplace-related outcomes such as: corporate citizenship behavior, turnover intentions, job stress, and job satisfaction any of which may act as antecedents of employee voice behavior. Besides contributing to achieve a better workplace for tomorrow by predicting proactive voice behavior of employees, the study has a potential to open new research avenues.

The next and the final section of this chapter will very briefly discuss the combined conclusion, managerial implications, and future research directions of all three independent empirical studies conducted in this dissertation.

4.5   Combined Conclusion, Managerial Implications and Future Research Directions

The whole study aimed to examine the relationship between employee personality, workplace mistreatment of employees carried out by their supervisors, and its impact on job outcomes. It was argued that employee personality may be depicted through their work ethics. Since the study was conducted in the context of Pakistan, which is an Islamic country, it was logical to consider Islamic work ethics (IWE) as a depiction of an individual's personality in the workplace. Employee's perceived abusive supervision, as proposed by Tepper (2000), was considered as a cognitive variable to represent workplace mistreatment.

By taking employee IWE and perceived abusive supervision into account, three independent empirical studies were carried out. In all of these studies, the impact of these variables was observed on the following workplace behaviors of employees: workplace deviance (WD) and prohibitive voice behavior (PVB).

The findings of the first study confirm that IWE is linked with lower WD. Also, WD is positively linked with employees' perceived abusive supervision. Additionally, when employees demonstrate a higher degree of deviant behavior, they attract more supervisory abuse. Thus, IWE plays a role in decreasing the level of employees' perceived supervisor abuse in the presence of WD. These results draw the focus of researchers and practitioners toward relatively less-explored predictors of perceived supervisory abuse in the workplace. Business managers could use these research findings to reduce the severity of perceived abusive supervision to make the workplace more productive and efficient.

Moreover, the findings of the second study confirm IWE as a predictor of workplace deviance. The relationship between IWE and workplace deviance is moderated by abusive supervision. Where, the same relationship is mediated by employee hostility. This study challenges a widely held research assumption. Previous researchers seemed to assume that IWE would always contribute either positively towards job outcomes that were to bring good, or would contribute to restrain outcomes that harm the organization. On the contrary, this study confirms there can be some situations when this assumption does not hold (e.g., in the presence of workplace mistreatment such as abusive supervision). Nevertheless, the results are still explainable within the teachings of Islam.

This research contributes in numerous ways. It identifies IWE as an antecedent of WD. It confirms the reversal of the conventional relationship between IWE and WD when employee perceived abusive supervision is high. The study verifies that employees' perceived abusive supervision moderates the relationship between IWE and WD. Besides, it confirms that the same relationship is mediated by employee hostility. With the help of these research findings, business managers can improve the workplace by reducing WD.

Lastly, the third study verifies the role played by IWE in predicting the voice behavior of employees. The findings confirm IWE is significantly and positively related to employees' prohibitive voice behavior (PVB). Employees who possess a higher degree of IWE strongly raise their voice in the workplace. Thus, employees who possess a higher degree of IWE are more likely to display PVB in the workplace. So, IWE can be considered as an antecedent of PVB. This voice behavior is a relatively less-explored job outcome in the context of Pakistan.

With the help of these research findings, business managers can promote organizational culture that can autocorrect the workplace. They can achieve favorable outcomes by placing employees with higher IWE in the organization. Consequently, by promoting PVB in the organization, decision-makers can formulate appropriate training or hiring plans.

The data for the studies were collected from 189 respondents working in or around Lahore, Pakistan. For better results, the research could include a larger number of respondents working in other parts of the country.

IWE have been discussed in all three studies. These work ethics possessed by subordinate might cause some consequences for supervisors and managers as well. Therefore, it might be interesting to see effect of subordinates' IWE on WD of supervisors or managers. In addition, the upcoming research could also test impact of IWE of supervisors or managers on deviant workplace behavior of their subordinates.

To increase generality of the study, future research could also use data collected from other Muslim countries to reproduce and confirm studies conducted in this dissertation. Future studies could also include other variables: self-esteem, organizational commitment, organizational citizenship behavior, self-efficacy, and emotional intelligence, which may moderate or mediate the relationship between IWE and WD. Some exciting results are expected to follow which can help improve the workplace of tomorrow.

4.6   Chapter Summary

Chapter 4 talked about the conclusion, managerial implications and future research directions of all the studies conducted in this dissertation. The first section, Section 4.1, very briefly introduced the structure of Chapter 4.

The next section, 4.2, revolved around Study 1: Islamic Work Ethics and Workplace Deviance: Antecedents of Abusive Supervision. The section 4.2 was further divided into three sub-sections: 4.2.1, 4.2.2, and 4.2.3. These sub- sections were respectively labeled as: Conclusion, Managerial implications and Future Research Directions of Study 1. These sub-sections highlighted some interesting aspects about conclusion, managerial implications and future research directions of Study 1.

Similarly, the next section, 4.3, revolved around Study 2: Islamic Work Ethics and Workplace Deviance: Moderated by Abusive Supervision and Mediated by Employee Hostility. This section 4.3 was further divided into three sub-sections: 4.3.1, 4.3.2, and 4.3.3. These sub- sections were respectively labeled as: Conclusion, Managerial implications and Future Research Directions of Study 2. These sub-sections highlighted some interesting aspects about conclusion, managerial implications and future research directions of Study 2.

Following the same pattern, the next section, 4.4 moved around Study 3: Study 3: Islamic Work Ethics and Employee Prohibitive Voice Behavior. The section 4.4 was further divided into three sub-sections: 4.4.1, 4.4.2, and 4.4.3. These sub-sections were respectively labeled as: Conclusion, Managerial implications and Future Research Directions of Study 3. All of these sub-sections highlighted some very interesting aspects about conclusion, managerial implications and future research directions of Study 3.

Finally, the next and the final section of this chapter, 4.5, very briefly discussed the combined conclusion, managerial implications, and future research directions of all three independent empirical studies conducted in this dissertation.

References

Abbas, M., Raja, U., Darr, W., & Bouckenooghe, D. (2014). Combined effects of perceived politics and psychological capital on job satisfaction, turnover intentions, and performance. *Journal of Management, 40*(7), 1813-1830.

Abuznaid, S. A. (2009). Business ethics in Islam: The glaring gap in practice. *International Journal of Islamic and Middle Eastern Finance and Management, 2*(4), 278-88.

Ahmad, A., & Omar, Z. (2014). Reducing deviant behavior through workplace spirituality and job satisfaction. *Asian Social Science, 10*(19), 107-112.

Ahmad, M. S. (2011). Work ethics: An Islamic prospective. *Journal of Human Sciences, 8*(1), 850-859.

Alarcon, G., Eschleman, K. J., & Bowling, N. A. (2009). Relationships between personality variables and burnout: A meta-analysis. *Work & Stress, 23*(3), 244-263.

Al-Bukhari, M. I. (1996). *The English Translation of Sahih Al Bukhari with the Arabic Text* (9 Volume Set). Translated by Muhammad Muhsin Khan, Al-Saadawi Publications.

Alhyasat, K. M. (2012). The role of Islamic work ethics in developing organizational citizenship behavior at the Jordanian press foundations. *Journal of Islamic Marketing, 3*(2), 139-54.

Ali, A. (1988). Scaling an Islamic work ethic. *The Journal of Social Psychology, 128*(5), 575-583.

Ali, A. J. (1992). The Islamic work ethic in Arabia. *The Journal of Psychology, 126*(5), 507-519.

Ali, A. J., & Al-Owaihan, A. (2008). Islamic work ethic: A critical review. *Cross cultural management. An International Journal, 15*(1), 5-19.

Ali, A.J. (2005). *Islamic perspectives on management and organization*. Edward Elgar.

Ali, A.J. (2015). *Handbook of research on Islamic business ethics*. Edward Elgar.

Aquino, K., & Bradfield, M. (2000). Perceived victimization in the workplace: The role of situational factors and victim characteristics. *Organization Science, 11*(5), 525-537.

Aquino, K., & Douglas, S. (2003). Identity threat and antisocial behavior in organizations: The moderating effects of individual differences, aggressive modeling, and hierarchical status. *Organizational Behavior and Human Decision Processes, 90*(1), 195-208.

Aquino, K., & Lamertz, K. (2004). A relational model of workplace victimization: Social roles and patterns of victimization in dyadic relationships. *Journal of Applied Psychology*, *89*(6), 1023-1034.

Aquino, K., & Thau, S. (2009). Workplace victimization: aggression from the target's perspective. *Annual Review of Psychology*, *60*, 717-741.

Arbuckle, J. L., & Wothke, W. (1999). *AMOS 4.0 user's guide*. Small Waters Corporation.

Arslan, M. (2000). A cross-cultural comparison of British and Turkish managers in terms of Protestant work ethic characteristics. *Business Ethics: A European Review*, *9*(1), 13-19.

Arslan, M. (2001). The work ethic values of protestant British, Catholic Irish and Muslim Turkish managers. *Journal of Business Ethics*, *31*(4), 321-339.

Artz, B., Goodall, A. H., & Oswald, A. J. (2020). How common are bad bosses? *Industrial Relations: A Journal of Economy and Society*, *59*(1), 3-39.

Barclay, L. J., Skarlicki, D. P., & Pugh, S. D. (2005). Exploring the role of emotions in injustice perceptions and retaliation. *Journal of Applied Psychology*, *90*(4), 629-643.

Bennett, R. J., & Robinson, S. L. (2000). Development of a measure of workplace deviance. *Journal of Applied Psychology*, *85*(3), 349-60.

Bentler, P. M., & Bonett, D. G. (1980). Significance tests and goodness of fit in the analysis of covariance structures. *Psychological Bulletin*, *88*(3), 588-606.

Bentler, Peter M. (1990). Comparative Fit Indexes in Structural Models. *Psychological Bulletin*, *107*(2), 238-46.

Bhatti, O. K., Alam, M. A., Hassan, A., & Sulaiman, M. (2016). Islamic spirituality and social responsibility in curtailing the workplace deviance. *Humanomics*, *32*(4), 405-417.

Bhatti, O. K., Alkahtani, A., Hassan, A., & Sulaiman, M. (2015). The relationship between Islamic piety (taqwa) and workplace deviance with organizational justice as a moderator. *International Journal of Business and Management*, *10*(4), 136-154.

Bijleveld, E., & Baalbergen, J. (2017). Prenatal exposure to testosterone (2D: 4D) and social hierarchy together predict voice behavior in bankers. *PloS One*, *12*(6), e0180008.

Bowling, N. A., & Eschleman, K. J. (2010). Employee personality as a moderator of the relationships between work stressors and counterproductive work behavior. *Journal of Occupational Health Psychology*, *15*(1), 91-103.

Bowling, N. A., Beehr, T. A., Bennett, M. M., & Watson, C. P. (2010). Target personality and workplace victimization: A prospective analysis. *Work & Stress*, *24*(2), 140-158.

Bratton, V. K., & Strittmatter, C. (2013). To cheat or not to cheat? The role of personality in academic and business ethics. *Ethics & Behavior, 23*(6), 427-444.

Brinsfield, C. T., Edwards, M. S., & Greenberg, J. (2009). Voice and silence in organizations: Historical review and current conceptualizations. In Jerald Greenberg and Marissa S. Edwards (Eds.), *Voice and silence in organizations*, Emeraled Group Publishing Limited, UK.

Buss, A. H., & Perry, M. (1992). The aggression questionnaire. *Journal of Personality and Social Psychology, 63*(3), 452-459.

Caspi, A., Roberts, B. W., & Shiner, R. L. (2005). Personality development: Stability and change. *Annual Review of Psychology, 56*, 453-484.

Chase-Dunn, C., Kawano, Y., & Brewer, B. D. (2000). Trade globalization since 1795: Waves of integration in the world-system. *American Sociological Review, 65*, 77-95.

Chen, F., Curran, P. J., Bollen, K. A., Kirby, J., & Paxton, P. (2008). An empirical evaluation of the use of fixed cutoff points in RMSEA test statistic in structural equation models. *Sociological Methods & Research, 36*(4), 462-494.

Chiaburu, D. S., Marinova, S. V., & Van Dyne, L. (2008). Should I do it or not? An initial model of cognitive processes predicting voice behaviors. In L. T. Kane & M. R. Poweller (Eds.), *Citizenship in the 21st Century*. Nova Science Publishers.

Cokley, K., Komarraju, M., Pickett, R., Shen, F., Patel, N., Belur, V., & Rosales, R. (2007). Ethnic differences in endorsement of the Protestant work ethic: The role of ethnic identity and perceptions of social class. *The Journal of Social Psychology, 147*(1), 75-89.

Colbert, A. E., Mount, M. K., Harter, J. K., Witt, L. A., & Barrick, M. R. (2004). Interactive effects of personality and perceptions of the work situation on workplace deviance. *Journal of Applied Psychology, 89*(4), 599-609.

Cole, D. A., Perkins, C. E., & Zelkowitz, R. L. (2016). Impact of homogeneous and heterogeneous parceling strategies when latent variables represent multidimensional constructs. *Psychological Methods, 21*(2), 164-174.

Comrey, A. L. (1978). Common methodological problems in factor analytic studies. *Journal of Consulting and Clinical Psychology, 46*(4), 648-659.

Conway, J. M., & Lance, C. E. (2010). What reviewers should expect from authors regarding common method bias in organizational research. *Journal of Business and Psychology, 25*(3), 325-334.

Cortina, L. M., Lonsway, K. A., Magley, V. J., Freeman, L. V., Collinsworth, L. L., Hunter, M., & Fitzgerald, L. F. (2002). What's gender got to do with it? Incivility in the federal courts. *Law & Social Inquiry, 27*(2), 235-270.

Crant, M. J. (2003). Speaking up when encouraged: Predicting voice behavior in a naturally-occurring setting. In *Annual Meeting of the Academy of Management*, Seattle.

De Clercq, D., Haq, I. U., Raja, U., Azeem, M. U., & Mahmud, N. (2018). When is an Islamic work ethic more likely to spur helping behavior? The roles of despotic leadership and gender. *Personnel Review, 47*(3), 630-650.

De Clercq, D., Rahman, Z., & Haq, I. U. (2019). Explaining helping behavior in the workplace: The interactive effect of family-to-work conflict and Islamic work ethic. *Journal of Business Ethics, 155*(4), 1167-1177.

Detert, J. R., & Burris, E. R. (2007). Leadership behavior and employee voice: Is the door really open? Academy of Management Journal, *50*(4), 869-884.

Duffy, M. K., Ganster, D. C., & Pagon, M. (2002). Social undermining in the workplace. *Academy of Management Journal, 45*(2), 331-351.

Dyne, L. V., Ang, S., & Botero, I. C. (2003). Conceptualizing employee silence and employee voice as multidimensional constructs. *Journal of Management Studies, 40*(6), 1359-1392.

Farid, T., Iqbal, S., Jawahar, I. M., Ma, J., & Khan, M. K. (2019). The interactive effects of justice perceptions and Islamic work ethic in predicting citizenship behaviors and work engagement. *Asian Business & Management, 18*(1), 31-50.

Ferris, D. L., Spence, J. R., Brown, D. J., & Heller, D. (2012). Interpersonal injustice and workplace deviance: The role of esteem threat. *Journal of Management, 38*(6), 1788-1811.

Fifka, M. S. (2013). Corporate citizenship in Germany and the United States–differing perceptions and practices in transatlantic comparison. *Business Ethics: A European Review, 22*(4), 341-356.

Fuller, J. B., Marler, L. E., & Hester, K. (2006). Promoting felt responsibility for constructive change and proactive behavior: Exploring aspects of an elaborated model of work design. *Journal of Organizational Behavior: The International Journal of Industrial, Occupational and Organizational Psychology and Behavior, 27*(8), 1089-1120.

Giorgi, L., & Marsh, C. (1990). The Protestant work ethic as a cultural phenomenon. *European Journal of Social Psychology, 20*(6), 499-517.

Golparvar, M., & Nadi, M. A. (2011). Mediating role of organizational loyalty in relation between work ethic with deviant workplace behavior. *Ethics in Science & Technology, 6*(1), 43-52.

Gouldner, A. W. (1960). The norm of reciprocity: A preliminary statement. *American Sociological Review, 25*(2), 161-178.

Haroon, M., Zaman, H. F., & Rehman, W. (2012). The relationship between Islamic work ethics and job satisfaction in healthcare sector of Pakistan. *International Journal of Contemporary Business Studies, 3*(5), 6-12.

Hassall, S. L., Muller, J. J., & Hassall, E. J. (2005). Comparing the Protestant work ethic in the employed and unemployed in Australia. *Journal of Economic Psychology, 26*(3), 327-341.

Hayati, K., & Caniago, I. (2012). Islamic work ethic: The role of intrinsic motivation, job satisfaction, organizational commitment and job performance. *Procedia-Social and Behavioral Sciences*, 65, 1102-1106.

Hayes, A. F., & Preacher, K. J. (2014). Statistical mediation analysis with a multi-categorical independent variable. *British Journal of Mathematical and Statistical Psychology*, 67(3), 451-470.

Henle, C. A., & Gross, M. A. (2014). What have I done to deserve this? Effects of employee personality and emotion on abusive supervision. *Journal of Business Ethics*, 122(3), 461-474.

Henle, C. A., Giacalone, R. A., & Jurkiewicz, C. L. (2005). The role of ethical ideology in workplace deviance. *Journal of Business Ethics*, 56(3), 219-230.

Hogler, R., Henle, C., & Gross, M. (2013). Ethical behavior and regional environments: The effects of culture, values, and trust. *Employee Responsibilities and Rights Journal*, 25(2), 109-121.

Homans, G. C. (1958). Social behavior as exchange. *American Journal of Sociology*, 63(6), 597-606.

Hu, L. T., & Bentler, P. M. (1999). Cutoff criteria for fit indexes in covariance structure analysis: Conventional criteria versus new alternatives. *Structural Equation Modeling: A Multidisciplinary Journal*, 6(1), 1-55.

Ibn-e-Majah (4004). *Sunan Ibn-e-Majah, Book of Hadith*: Darussalam Publications.

Javed, B., Fatima, T., Yasin, R. M., Jahanzeb, S., & Rawwas, M. Y. (2019). Impact of abusive supervision on deviant work behavior: The role of Islamic work ethic. *Business Ethics: A European Review*, 28(2), 221-233.

Johnson, T. M., & Grim, B. J. (2013). *The world's religions in figures: A introduction to international religious demography*. John Wiley & Sons.

Judge, B. (2002). Ilies & Gerhardt (2002), Personality and leadership: A quantitative review. *Journal of Applied Psychology*, 87(4), 765-780.

Judge, T. A., Bono, J. E., & Locke, E. A. (2000). Personality and job satisfaction: The mediating role of job characteristics. *Journal of Applied Psychology*, 85(2), 237-249.

Khalid, F., Mirza, S. S., Bin-Feng, C., & Saeed, N. (2020). Learning engagements and the role of religion. *SAGE Open*, 10(1), 1-14.

Khan, A. K., Moss, S., Quratulain, S., & Hameed, I. (2018). When and how subordinate performance leads to abusive supervision: A social dominance perspective. *Journal of Management*, 44(7), 2801-2826.

Khan, A. K., Quratulain, S., & Crawshaw, J. R. (2017). Double jeopardy: Subordinates' worldviews and poor performance as predictors of abusive supervision. *Journal of Business and Psychology*, 32(2), 165-178.

Khan, K., Abbas, M., Gul, A., & Raja, U. (2015). Organizational justice and job outcomes: Moderating role of Islamic work ethic. *Journal of Business Ethics, 126*(2), 235-246.

Kim, E., & Glomb, T. M. (2010). Get smarty pants: Cognitive ability, personality, and victimization. *Journal of Applied Psychology, 95*(5), 889-901.

Kline, R. B. (2015). *Principles and practice of structural equation modeling.* Guilford Publications.

Kumar, N., & Rose, R. C. (2010). Examining the link between Islamic work ethic and innovation capability. *Journal of Management Development, 29*(1), 79-93.

Kumar, N., & Rose, R. C. (2012). The impact of knowledge sharing and Islamic work ethic on innovation capability. *Cross Cultural Management: An International Journal, 19*(2), 142-65.

LePine, J. A., & Van Dyne, L. (1998). Predicting voice behavior in work groups. *Journal of Applied Psychology, 83*(6), 853-68.

LePine, J. A., & Van Dyne, L. (2001). Voice and cooperative behavior as contrasting forms of contextual performance: Evidence of differential relationships with big five personality characteristics and cognitive ability. *Journal of Applied Psychology, 86*(2), 326-336.

Lewis, M. (2011). *Ethical principles in Islamic business and banking transactions.* Edward Elgar Publishing.

Li, X., Qian, J., Han, Z. R., & Jin, Z. (2016). Coping with abusive supervision: The neutralizing effects of perceived organizational support and political skill on employees' burnout. *Current Psychology, 35*(1), 77-82.

Liang, J., Farh, C. I., & Farh, J. L. (2012). Psychological antecedents of promotive and prohibitive voice: A two-wave examination. *Academy of Management Journal, 55*(1), 71-92.

Liu, W., Zhang, P., Liao, J., Hao, P. and Mao, J. (2016). Abusive supervision and employee creativity: The mediating role of psychological safety and organizational identification, *Management Decision, 54*(1), 130-147.

Luna-Arocas, R., & Tang, T. L. P. (2004). The love of money, satisfaction, and the protestant work ethic: Money profiles among university professors in the USA and Spain. *Journal of Business Ethics, 50*(4), 329-354.

Maoz, Z., & Henderson, E. A. (2013). The world religion dataset, 1945–2010: Logic, estimates, and trends. *International Interactions, 39*(3), 265-291.

Marri, M. Y. K., Sadozai, A. M., Zaman, H. M. F., & Ramay, M. I. (2012). The impact of Islamic work ethics on job satisfaction and organizational commitment: a study of agriculture sector of Pakistan. *International Journal of Business and Behavioral Sciences, 2*(12), 32-45.

Marsh, H. W., Hau, K. T., & Wen, Z. (2004). In search of golden rules: Comment on hypothesis-testing approaches to setting cutoff values for fit indexes and dangers in overgeneralizing Hu and Bentler's (1999) findings. *Structural Equation Modeling, 11*(3), 320-341.

Mathieu, C., & Babiak, P. (2016). Corporate psychopathy and abusive supervision: Their influence on employees' job satisfaction and turnover intentions. *Personality and Individual Differences, 91*, 102-106.

Mawritz, M. B., Greenbaum, R. L., Butts, M. M., & Graham, K. A. (2017). I just can't control myself: A self-regulation perspective on the abuse of deviant employees. *Academy of Management Journal, 60*(4), 1482-1503.

Mayer, D. M., Thau, S., Workman, K. M., Van Dijke, M., & De Cremer, D. (2012). Leader mistreatment, employee hostility, and deviant behaviors: Integrating self-uncertainty and thwarted needs perspectives on deviance. *Organizational Behavior and Human Decision Processes, 117*(1), 24-40.

Minhat, M., & Dzolkarnaini, N. (2016). Islamic corporate financing: does it promote profit and loss sharing? *Business Ethics: A European Review, 25*(4), 482-497.

Mitchell, M. S., & Ambrose, M. L. (2007). Abusive supervision and workplace deviance and the moderating effects of negative reciprocity beliefs. *Journal of Applied Psychology, 92*(4), 1159-1168.

Moayedi, N. N. (2009). *Islamic work ethic and Muslim religious beliefs impact on organizational commitment in the workplace* [Unpublished doctoral dissertation]. University of Phoenix.

Mohammad, J., & Quoquab, F. (2016). Furthering the thought on Islamic work ethic: how does it differ? *Journal of Islamic Marketing, 7*(3), 355-375.

Mohammad, J., Quoquab, F., Idris, F., Al-Jabari, M., Hussin, N., & Wishah, R. (2018). The relationship between Islamic work ethic and workplace outcome. *Personnel Review, 47*(7), 1286-1308.

Mowday, R. T., & Spencer, D. G. (1981). The influence of task and personality characteristics on employee turnover and absenteeism incidents. *Academy of Management Journal, 24*(3), 634-642.

Mursaleen, M., Saqib, L., Roberts, K. W., & Asif, M. (2015). Islamic work ethics as mediator between trust and knowledge sharing relationship. *Pakistan Journal of Commerce and Social Sciences* (PJCSS), *9*(2), 614-640.

Murtaza, G., Abbas, M., Raja, U., Roques, O., Khalid, A., & Mushtaq, R. (2016). Impact of Islamic work ethics on organizational citizenship behaviors and knowledge-sharing behaviors. *Journal of Business Ethics, 133*(2), 325-333.

Neves, P. (2014). Taking it out on survivors: Submissive employees, downsizing, and abusive supervision. *Journal of Occupational and Organizational Psychology, 87*(3), 507-534.

Niles, F. S. (1999). Toward a cross-cultural understanding of work-related beliefs. *Human Relations, 52*(7), 855-867.

Nixon, D. (2009). I can't put a smiley face on': Working-class masculinity, emotional labour and service work in the 'New Economy. *Gender, Work & Organization, 16*(3), 300-322.

O'Neill, T. A., Lewis, R. J., & Carswell, J. J. (2011). Employee personality, justice perceptions, and the prediction of workplace deviance. *Personality and Individual Differences, 51*(5), 595-600.

Parasuraman, A., Berry, L., & Zeithaml, V. (2002). Refinement and reassessment of the SERVQUAL scale. *Journal of Retailing, 67*(4), 114-139.

Parboteeah, K. P., Paik, Y., & Cullen, J. B. (2009). Religious groups and work values: A focus on Buddhism, Christianity, Hinduism, and Islam. *International Journal of Cross Cultural Management, 9*(1), 51-67.

Park, J. W., Robertson, R., & Wu, C. L. (2006). Modelling the impact of airline service quality and marketing variables on passengers' future behavioural intentions. *Transportation Planning and Technology, 29*(5), 359-381.

Parker, S. K., & Collins, C. G. (2010). Taking stock: Integrating and differentiating multiple proactive behaviors. *Journal of Management, 36*(3), 633-662.

Peng, H., & Wei, F. (2019). How and when does leader behavioral integrity influence employee voice? The roles of team independence climate and corporate ethical values. *Journal of Business Ethics, 5*(1), 1-17.

Podsakoff, N. P. (2003). Common method biases in behavioral research: a critical review of the literature and recommended remedies. *Journal of Applied Psychology, 88*(5), 879-903.

Porter, G. (2005). A "career" work ethic versus just a job. *Journal of European Industrial Training, 29*(4), 336-352.

Premeaux, S. F., & Bedeian, A. G. (2003). Breaking the silence: The moderating effects of self-monitoring in predicting speaking up in the workplace. *Journal of Management Studies, 40*(6), 1537-1562.

Qur'an (1981). Arabic text and English translation. Islamic Seminary, Elmhurst, NY, USA.

Raja, U., Johns, G., & Ntalianis, F. (2004). The impact of personality on psychological contracts. *Academy of Management Journal, 47*(3), 350-367.

Rawwas, M. Y., Javed, B., & Iqbal, M. N. (2018). Perception of politics and job outcomes: moderating role of Islamic work ethic. *Personnel Review, 47*(1), 74-94.

Rice, G. (1999). Islamic ethics and the implications for business. *Journal of Business Ethics, 18*(4), 345-358.

Robinson, S. L., & Bennett, R. J. (1995). A typology of deviant workplace behaviors: A multidimensional scaling study. *Academy of Management Journal, 38*(2), 555-572.

Rokhman, W. (2010). The effect of Islamic work ethics on work outcomes. *EJBO-Electronic Journal of Business Ethics and Organization Studies, 15*(1), 21-27.

Saheeh International (1997). *The Holy Qur'an: Arabic text with corresponding English meanings*. Abul-Qasim Publishing House.

Sahih Muslim by Imam Muslim, translation by Abdul Hamid Siddiqui.

Saks, A. M., Mudrack, P. E., & Ashforth, B. E. (1996). The relationship between the work ethic, job attitudes, intentions to quit, and turnover for temporary service employees. *Canadian Journal of Administrative Sciences/Revue Canadienne des Sciences de l'Administration, 13*(3), 226-236.

Salin, D. (2003). Ways of explaining workplace bullying: A review of enabling, motivating and precipitating structures and processes in the work environment. *Human Relations, 56*(10), 1213-1232.

Schermelleh-Engel, K., Moosbrugger, H., & Müller, H. (2003). Evaluating the fit of structural equation models: Tests of significance and descriptive goodness-of-fit measures. *Methods of Psychological Research Online, 8*(2), 23-74.

Sheehy, J. W. (1990). New work ethic is frightening. *Personnel Journal, 69*(6), 28-36.

Smith, M. B., & Webster, B. D. (2017). A moderated mediation model of Machiavellianism, social undermining, political skill, and supervisor-rated job performance. *Personality and Individual Differences, 104*, 453-459.

Spector, P. E., Fox, S., Penney, L. M., Bruursema, K., Goh, A., & Kessler, S. (2006). The dimensionality of counter productivity: Are all counterproductive behaviors created equal? *Journal of Vocational Behavior, 68*(3), 446-460.

Syed, N. A., & Azam, A. (2019). Islamic work ethics and workplace deviance: Moderating role of employees' perceived abusive supervision and mediating role of employees' hostility. *Pakistan Journal of Commerce and Social Sciences (PJCSS), 13*(4), 952-975.

Tayeb, M. (1997). Islamic revival in Asia and human resource management. *Employee Relations, 19*(4), 352-364.

Tepper, B. J. (2000). Consequences of abusive supervision. *Academy of Management Journal, 43*(2), 178-190.

Tepper, B. J. (2007). Abusive supervision in work organizations: Review, synthesis, and research agenda. *Journal of Management, 33*(3), 261-289.

Tepper, B. J., Carr, J. C., Breaux, D. M., Geider, S., Hu, C., & Hua, W. (2009). Abusive supervision, intentions to quit, and employees' workplace deviance: A power/dependence analysis. *Organizational Behavior and Human Decision Processes, 109*(2), 156-167.

Tepper, B. J., Duffy, M. K., Henle, C. A., & Lambert, L. S. (2006). Procedural injustice, victim precipitation, and abusive supervision. *Personnel Psychology, 59*(1), 101-123.

Tepper, B. J., Henle, C. A., Lambert, L. S., Giacalone, R. A., & Duffy, M. K. (2008). Abusive supervision and subordinates' organization deviance. *Journal of Applied Psychology, 93*(4), 721-732.

Tepper, B. J., Moss, S. E., & Duffy, M. K. (2011). Predictors of abusive supervision: Supervisor perceptions of deep-level dissimilarity, relationship conflict, and subordinate performance. *Academy of Management Journal, 54*(2), 279-294.

Thau, S., Bennett, R. J., Mitchell, M. S., & Marrs, M. B. (2009). How management style moderates the relationship between abusive supervision and workplace deviance: An uncertainty management theory perspective. *Organizational Behavior and Human Decision Processes, 108*(1), 79-92.

Thomas, J. P., Whitman, D. S., & Viswesvaran, C. (2010). Employee proactivity in organizations: A comparative meta-analysis of emergent proactive constructs. *Journal of Occupational and Organizational Psychology, 83*(2), 275-300.

Treviño, L. K., Weaver, G. R., & Reynolds, S. J. (2006). Behavioral ethics in organizations: A review. *Journal of Management, 32*(6), 951-990.

Uygur, S. (2009). The Islamic work ethic and the emergence of Turkish SME owner-managers. *Journal of Business Ethics, 88*(1), 211-225.

Walker, L. J., & Frimer, J. A. (2007). Moral personality of brave and caring exemplars. *Journal of Personality and Social Psychology, 93*(5), 845-860.

Weber, M. (2013). *The Protestant Ethic and the Spirit of Capitalism*. Routledge.

Weiss, H. M., & Cropanzano, R. (1996). Affective events theory: A theoretical discussion of the structure, causes and consequences of affective experiences at work. *Research in Organizational Behavior, 18*, 1-74.

Wolfgang, M. E. (1957). Victim precipitated criminal homicide. *The Journal of Criminal Law, Criminology, and Police Science, 48*(1), 1-11.

Wu, T. Y., & Hu, C. (2013). Abusive supervision and subordinate emotional labor: The moderating role of openness personality. *Journal of Applied Social Psychology, 43*(5), 956-970.

Yousef, D. A. (2000a). The Islamic work ethic as a mediator of the relationship between locus of control, role conflict and role ambiguity–A study in an Islamic country setting. *Journal of Managerial Psychology, 15*(4), 283-298.

Yousef, D. A. (2000b). Organizational commitment as a mediator of the relationship between Islamic work ethic and attitudes toward organizational change. *Human Relations, 53*(4), 513-537.

Yousef, D. A. (2001). Islamic work ethic–A moderator between organizational commitment and job satisfaction in a cross-cultural context. *Personnel Review, 30*(2), 152-69.

Zapf, D., Einarsen, S., Hoel, H., & Vartia, M. (2003). Empirical findings on bullying in the workplace. In S. Einarsen, H. Hoel, D. Zapf & C.L. Cooper (Eds.), *Bullying and emotional abuse in the workplace: International perspectives in research and practice* (pp. 103-126). Taylor & Francis.

Zellars, K. L., Tepper, B. J., & Duffy, M. K. (2002). Abusive supervision and subordinates' organizational citizenship behavior. *Journal of Applied Psychology, 87*(6), 1068-1076.

Appendix

Set of Questionnaires

SUPERVISOR'S GENERAL PERCEPTIONS

COMPANY'S INFORMATION

Form A

Name of Manager/Supervisor: ______________________________

Name of the company: ______________________________

Number of employees in the company: ☐ 0-25   ☐ 26-100   ☐ 101-500
☐ 501-1000   ☐ More than 1000

The industry your company belongs to:

☐ Pharmaceuticals, Biotechnology

☐ Agriculture

☐ Textiles, Garments, Leather Goods, Sports Goods

☐ Paper and Packaging

☐ Fertilizers, Chemicals, Sugar, Cement

☐ Light Engineering (Auto Parts, Electrical Appliances etc.)

☐ Heavy Engineering (Machinery, Automobiles, Motorcycles etc.)

☐ Service Industry (Banking, Software, Telecom etc.)

☐ Other (Specify): __________

SUPERVISOR'S INFORMATION

Gender: ☐ Male   ☐ Female

Age: ☐ Less than 25   ☐ 25-30   ☐ 31-34   ☐ 35-40
☐ 41-44   ☐ 45-50   ☐ 51-54   ☐ 55 and above

Qualification: ☐ Intermediate   ☐ Bachelors   ☐ Masters   ☐ Doctorate

Experience (current organization):
☐ Less than 5 years   ☐ 6-10 years   ☐ 11-15 years   ☐ More than 15 years

Hierarchical Level: ☐ Entry level   ☐ Middle level   ☐ Senior level

Department: ☐ Administration   ☐ Human Resource   ☐ Finance &Accounts
☐ Sales   ☐Opreations   ☐ Marketing
☐ Information Technology
☐ Other: __________________

SUPERVISOR'S PERCEPTION ABOUT SUBORDINATE

Employee Name (for whom this form is filled): _______________________________________

Please rate this **<u>SUBORDINATE</u>** on the following statements.

Assigned Code: 1

Please indicate your response by selecting the appropriate number.	Unacceptable	Below Average	Average	Above Average	Outstanding
Rate the overall level of performance that you observe for this subordinate.	1	2	3	4	5
Please indicate your response by selecting the appropriate number.	1	2	3	4	5
What is your personal view of this subordinate in terms of his or her overall effectiveness?	1	2	3	4	5
Please indicate your response by selecting the appropriate number.	1	2	3	4	5
Overall, to what extent do you feel this subordinate has been effectively fulfilling his or her roles and responsibilities?	1	2	3	4	5
Please indicate the degree of your agreement/disagreement by selecting the appropriate number.	1	2	3	4	5
My subordinate is superior to other subordinates that I have supervised before.	1	2	3	4	5

Form B-I

SUBORDINATE'S SURVEY

Name:_______________________

Assigned Code:_______________

NOTE
- Please keep this form confidential and do not show it to anyone.
- Anonymity of the responses is assured and the information being collected will remain confidential.

Below are a series of statements with which you may either agree or disagree. For each statement, please indicate the degree of your agreement/disagreement by selecting the appropriate number.

For each statement, please indicate the degree of your agreement/disagreement by selecting the appropriate number.		Strongly Disagree	Disagree	Neither Agree Nor Disagree	Agree	Strongly Agree
1.	Laziness is a vice (defect).	1	2	3	4	5
2.	Dedication to work is a virtue (good behavior).	1	2	3	4	5
3.	Good work benefits both one's self and others.	1	2	3	4	5
4.	Justice and generosity in the work place are necessary conditions for society's welfare.	1	2	3	4	5
5.	Producing more than enough to meet one's personal needs contributes to the prosperity of society as a whole.	1	2	3	4	5
6.	One should carry work out to the best of one's ability.	1	2	3	4	5
7.	Work is not an end in itself but a means to foster personal growth and social relations.	1	2	3	4	5
8.	Life has no meaning without work.	1	2	3	4	5
9.	More leisure time is good for society.	1	2	3	4	5
10.	Human relations in organizations should be emphasized and encouraged.	1	2	3	4	5
11.	Work enables man to control nature.	1	2	3	4	5
12.	Creative work is a source of happiness and accomplishment.	1	2	3	4	5
13.	Any man who works is more likely to get ahead in life.	1	2	3	4	5
14.	Work gives one the chance to be independent.	1	2	3	4	5
15.	A successful man is the one who meets deadlines at work.	1	2	3	4	5
16.	One should constantly work hard to meet responsibilities.	1	2	3	4	5
17.	The value of work is derived from the accompanying intentions rather than the results.	1	2	3	4	5

For each statement, please indicate the degree of your agreement/disagreement by selecting the appropriate number.	Strongly Disagree	Disagree	Neither Agree Nor Disagree	Agree	Strongly Agree
1. I am sometimes eaten up with (controlled by) jealousy.	1	2	3	4	5
2. At times I feel I have gotten a raw deal (unfair treatment) out of life.	1	2	3	4	5
3. Other people always seem to get the breaks (opportunities).	1	2	3	4	5
4. I wonder why sometimes I feel so bitter about things.	1	2	3	4	5
5. I know that "friends/colleagues" talk about me behind my back.	1	2	3	4	5
6. I am suspicious of overly friendly strangers.	1	2	3	4	5
7. I sometimes feel that people are laughing at me behind my back.	1	2	3	4	5
8. When people are especially (more than ever) nice, I wonder what they want.	1	2	3	4	5

For each statement, please indicate the degree of your agreement/disagreement by selecting the appropriate number.	Strongly Disagree	Disagree	Neither Agree Nor Disagree	Agree	Strongly Agree
1. My supervisor ridicules me.	1	2	3	4	5
2. My supervisor tells me my thoughts or feelings are stupid.	1	2	3	4	5
3. My supervisor gives me the silent treatment.	1	2	3	4	5
4. My supervisor puts me down in front of others.	1	2	3	4	5
5. My supervisor invades my privacy.	1	2	3	4	5
6. My supervisor reminds me of my past mistakes and failures.	1	2	3	4	5
7. My supervisor doesn't give me credit for jobs requiring a lot of effort.	1	2	3	4	5
8. My supervisor blames me for his or her own mistakes.	1	2	3	4	5
9. My supervisor breaks promises he or she makes.	1	2	3	4	5
10. My supervisor expresses anger at me when he or she is mad for another reason.	1	2	3	4	5
11. My supervisor makes negative comments about me to others.	1	2	3	4	5
12. My supervisor is rude to me.	1	2	3	4	5
13. My supervisor does not allow me to interact with my coworkers.	1	2	3	4	5
14. My supervisor tells me I am incompetent.	1	2	3	4	5
15. My supervisor lies to me.	1	2	3	4	5

For each statement, please indicate the degree of your agreement/disagreement by selecting the appropriate number.	Strongly Disagree	Disagree	Neither Agree Nor Disagree	Agree	Strongly Agree
1. I am strong enough to overcome life's struggles.	1	2	3	4	5
2. At root (basically), I am a weak person.	1	2	3	4	5
3. I can handle the situations that life brings.	1	2	3	4	5
4. I usually feel that I am an unsuccessful person.	1	2	3	4	5
5. I often feel that there is nothing that I can do well.	1	2	3	4	5
6. I feel competent to deal effectively with the real world.	1	2	3	4	5
7. I often feel like a failure.	1	2	3	4	5
8. I usually feel I can handle the typical problems that come up in life.	1	2	3	4	5

EMPLOYEE INFORMATION

Gender: ☐ Male ☐ Female

Age: ☐ Less than 25 years ☐ 25-30 years ☐ 31-34 years ☐ 35-40 years
☐ 41-44 years ☐ 45-50 years ☐ 51-54 years ☐ 55 years and above

Qualification: ☐ Intermediate ☐ Bachelors ☐ Masters ☐ Doctorate

Experience (current organization)
☐ Less than 5 years ☐ 6-10 years ☐ 11-15 years ☐ More than 15 years

Hierarchical Level:
☐ Entry level ☐ Middle level ☐ Senior level

Time spent under current supervisor:
☐ Less than a year ☐ 1 - 2 years ☐ 3 - 5 years ☐ 6 - 10 years
☐ More than 10 years

Form B-II

SUBORDINATE'S SURVEY

Name:_____________________

Assigned Code:_____________

NOTE
- Please keep this form confidential and do not show it to anyone.
- Anonymity of the responses is assured and the information being collected will remain confidential.

Below are a series of statements with which you may either agree or disagree. For each statement, please indicate the degree of your agreement/disagreement by selecting the appropriate number.

	For each statement, please indicate the degree of your agreement/disagreement by selecting the appropriate number.	Strongly Disagree	Disagree	Neither Agree Nor Disagree	Agree	Strongly Agree
1.	I make fun of someone at work.	1	2	3	4	5
2.	I say something hurtful/painful to someone at work.	1	2	3	4	5
3.	I make an ethnic, religious, or racial remark at work.	1	2	3	4	5
4.	I curse at someone at work.	1	2	3	4	5
5.	I play a mean prank (joke) on someone at work.	1	2	3	4	5
6.	I act rudely towards someone at work.	1	2	3	4	5
7.	I publicly embarrass someone at work.	1	2	3	4	5
8.	I take property from work without permission.	1	2	3	4	5
9.	I spend too much time fantasizing or daydreaming instead of working.	1	2	3	4	5
10.	I falsify a receipt to get reimbursed for more money than I spent on business expenses.	1	2	3	4	5
11.	I take an additional or longer break than is acceptable at my workplace.	1	2	3	4	5
12.	I come in late to work without permission.	1	2	3	4	5
13.	I litter (throw garbage in) my work environment.	1	2	3	4	5
14.	I neglect to follow my supervisor's instructions.	1	2	3	4	5
15.	I intentionally work slower than I could have worked.	1	2	3	4	5
16.	I discuss confidential company information with an unauthorized person.	1	2	3	4	5
17.	I use an illegal drug or consumed alcohol on the job.	1	2	3	4	5
18.	I put little effort into my work.	1	2	3	4	5
19.	I drag out (delay) work in order to get overtime.	1	2	3	4	5

For each statement, please indicate the degree of your agreement/disagreement by selecting the appropriate number.	Strongly Disagree	Disagree	Neither Agree Nor Disagree	Agree	Strongly Agree
1. All in all, I am satisfied with my job.	1	2	3	4	5
2. In general, I like working here.	1	2	3	4	5
3. My job is enjoyable.	1	2	3	4	5
4. I feel a sense of pride in doing my job.	1	2	3	4	5
5. In general, I don't like my job.	1	2	3	4	5

For each statement, please indicate the degree of your agreement/disagreement by selecting the appropriate number.	Strongly Disagree	Disagree	Neither Agree Nor Disagree	Agree	Strongly Agree
1. I advise other colleagues against undesirable behaviors that would hamper job performance.	1	2	3	4	5
2. I speak up honestly with problems that might cause serious loss to the organization, even when dissenting (disagreeing) opinions exist.	1	2	3	4	5
3. I dare to voice out opinions on things that might affect efficiency in the organization, even if that would embarrass others.	1	2	3	4	5
4. I dare to point out problems when they appear in the organization, even if that would hamper relationships with other colleagues.	1	2	3	4	5
5. I proactively report coordination problems in the workplace to the management.	1	2	3	4	5